The Dark Night of
SAMUEL TAYLOR COLERIDGE

The Dark Night of
SAMUEL TAYLOR COLERIDGE

By MARSHALL SUTHER

New York 1960
COLUMBIA UNIVERSITY PRESS

N.C.
821.09
S

To Elizabeth Ewing

ACKNOWLEDGMENTS

I should like to express my appreciation to copyright holders and publishers for permission to quote from the following works: Cahiers du Sud, for *L'Ame Romantique et le Reve,* Vol. I, by Albert Beguin; Harcourt, Brace and Company, for *Collected Poems* by T. S. Eliot; Alfred A. Knopf, for *Selected Poems* by John Crowe Ransom; The Macmillan Company, for *Collected Poems* by W. B. Yeats; Scribner's, for *The Spirit of Medieval Philosophy* by Etienne Gilson; Scribner's and Sheed & Ward Ltd., for *Art and Scholasticism* by Jacques Maritian; The Philosophical Library, for *The Situation of Poetry* by Jacques and Raïssa Maritain; Random House, for "A Poem of Pure Imagination," copyright 1946 by Robert Penn Warren, reprinted from *Selected Essays* by Robert Penn Warren.

New York, 1960   MARSHALL SUTHER

CONTENTS

The Dark Night of
SAMUEL TAYLOR COLERIDGE

INTRODUCTION

This book is concerned with what those acquainted with Coleridge criticism may consider the well-worn subject of the "Coleridge riddle"—the question, what happened to Coleridge? Or rather, Why did it happen? The original impetus for undertaking it came from the reading of two works, Coleridge's own "Dejection: An Ode," and a book by Jacques and Raïssa Maritain, *The Situation of Poetry*,[1] which in turn led to two works by Albert Béguin, *L'Ame Romantique et le Rêve*[2] and *Poésie et Mystique*.[3] These recent works, written without any reference to Coleridge, suggested avenues of research in his own life and works which might be enlightening to the student still puzzled by the apparent anomalies of Coleridge's career.

There seems to be very nearly universal agreement as to Coleridge's intellectual stature: he possessed one of the most agile and comprehensive minds we know of in nineteenth-century England. Students of the nineteenth century now recognize his tremendous influence on subsequent thought—through the medium of works that no one except those students ever reads, and through his conversation. A half-dozen or so of his poems are singled out by the widest variety of critics (from John Livingston

[1] New York: Philosophical Library, 1955.
[2] Marseille: Editions des Cahiers du Sud, 1937, 2 vols.
[3] Appendix to *Gérard de Nerval* (Paris: Librairie Stock, 1936).

Lowes to Robert Penn Warren) as among the first in the language, and these half-dozen represent a variety of forms indicative of a major, not a minor poet. As philosopher-psychologist-critic he has in recent years received as impressive recognition as he received from a large number of his contemporaries. I refer especially to the works of I. A. Richards and J. H. Muirhead, but to consult the indexes of a random selection of recent works treating directly or indirectly the history of thought is in a way even more striking. In fact, so great is the impression of power received from fresh contact with Coleridge's poetry and his prose when approached in the absence of the stock formulas about "romantic poets," that critics now not infrequently suggest that nothing happened to him at all, that an intelligent re-reading of his poetry would result in the discovery of well over half a dozen great poems, that his philosophical, psychological, and critical works need only a little reorganizing to be seen as finished monuments of thought. In short, there has been a kind of Coleridge "boom" in progress, and Richards, for instance, is rather sharply impatient with apologizers for Coleridge.

But although, as Richards says, "The literature on his 'case' must by now be nearly as voluminous as his own writings," and in spite of the facts previously mentioned, there does appear to be a "case," a riddle, and although it is probably not the kind of riddle that can be solved, attempts to clarify its terms can be illuminating. Although it is true that Coleridge's poems will repay closer attention, and a different kind of reading, than they have often received (witness Robert Penn Warren's impressive performance on *The Ancient Mariner*[4]), it is also true that his recognizedly greatest poems were written within a few years in

---

[4] "A Poem of Pure Imagination, an Experiment in Reading," in *The Rime of the Ancient Mariner, with an Essay by Robert Penn Warren* (New York: Reynal & Hitchcock, 1946).

his youth, and that, however misprized his later poems may have been, they do not measure up to the order of promise of the great early ones. Of this fact Coleridge himself is the first witness. The position may be put in the form of a question: What other poet in English literature wrote a poem seriously comparable with *The Ancient Mariner* by the time he was twenty-five and never succeeded in finishing another one on anything like the same scale throughout a long lifetime? Although one might not quarrel even with a statement that Coleridge's philosophical works are more interesting than those of any other nineteenth-century Englishman, it is also true that all of his immense erudition and fresh creative insight did not issue in a "work"—much less in a "system" (although Coleridge himself never ceased to the day of his death to lament his failure to establish "his system").

And so we have a man of first promise both as poet and as philosopher, who, though he worked hard through a long lifetime (the myth of his laziness has long since been discredited by the mere volume of his written works), fell dramatically short of that promise, the flow of his poetic inspiration drying up almost suddenly, his philosophy never coming to anything like a definitive form, a prey throughout his life to serious depression, a "confirmed" opium addict, and, in the eyes of some of his ablest friends and of numerous subsequent critics, a failure—in spite of his achievements—because of his promise. Perhaps Richards ought to be a little easier on all the people who have scrutinized Coleridge's life with a view to praise, blame, or excuse. Their preoccupation with Coleridge is different from his, but perhaps not less significant or interesting. The fact that so much of this examination has gone on, and continues to this date, is indicative of the peculiar stature of Coleridge as a whole person, rather than as poet, as philosopher, or as critic. People are usually examined in this way because they appear to have lived through certain basic, perennial problems in a unique and revelatory way.[5] If Coleridge is still a subject of debate, one reason is that a hundred and fifty years ago he was already grappling brilliantly and unsuccessfully with what are still crucial problems of artistic, philosophical, and religious adjustment, problems which few if any of his contemporaries grasped as directly as he did.

An understanding of "What happened to Coleridge" can only be approached through keeping in view *the man Coleridge,* who is more than the sum of what we can formulate as his artistic interests, his philosophical tendencies, his personal emotional conflicts, a man whose over-all "problem" can only be seen, finally, as a religious one, as that of a highly conscious soul in struggle with its spiritual destiny, using every tool, every virtue, and even every vice, at its command.

This is a disquieting kind of terminology to embark upon. But the tendency, evident in much that has been written about Coleridge, to reduce him to the dimensions of one of his talents, and to minimize its conflicts with the others, the tacit refusal to consider the obvious and heroic paradox of his life, stems itself perhaps from what may be called a positivist bias, a disinclination to recognize the existence, or in any case the pertinence, of any disorder which cannot be diagnosed and dealt with in the terms of certain accepted disciplines, preferably scientific ones like medicine or clinical psychology, or at least sane ones like philoso-

---

[5] It may even be true, as Richards suggests in a recent article, "Coleridge, the Vulnerable Poet," *Yale Review* XLVIII (New Series: June, 1959), 491-504, that some studies of Coleridge say more about their authors than they do about Coleridge, but it does not follow that this is a complete loss from our point of view, or, if it is relevant, that Coleridge would be displeased by the fact. Although only one of his works is entitled *Aids to Reflection,* it is permissible to think that his dearest wish was that all of his works might, in fact, deserve such a title.

phy or criticism. This bias must certainly eliminate a good deal of sheer romancing and pompous rhetoric—though it also produces some rather ridiculous monstrosities in the form of clinical "explanations." Insofar as it is the result of a drive toward procedural rigor and proper philosophical modesty, the positivist bias is unquestionably salutary.

But a certain naïve candor forces us to recognize that in this process of reduction the *man* tends to disappear. Beyond the boundaries of consideration as they are now frequently drawn, it may well be that the problems and the solutions to them become vaguer, more difficult to seize, formulate, and use. *A soul in struggle with its destiny* is not nearly so tractable a conception as *a sufferer from schizophrenia* or even *a philosopher confused by a certain imbalance, leading him to irrelevant theological speculations*. The fact is that Coleridge himself did not draw back, but resisted with all his force the tendency to assume in the phenomena under consideration those limits which really derive from our methods of considering. When terms and concepts seemed to be lacking, he refined old ones and invented new ones (some of them brilliant strokes of insight, some of them compounding confusion). His greatness lies precisely in his dogged refusal to pretend that the problems and paradoxes of human life are any less vast, ineffable, and terrifying than his intuition revealed to him they were. In his struggle to come to terms with life as he found it, the phenomena referred to by the aid of words like "tragedy," "sin," "guilt," "redemption," "grace," "Reason," "inspiration," and "God," were immediate factors, though no one recognized more clearly than he that each one of them as a possessed conception was infinitely inadequate to name the phenomenon to which it pointed. His *philosophical* effort was to refine those conceptions by means of good logical pro-

cedure and constant reference to his experience of their correspondents—not to reduce them, and, by implication, their corresponding phenomena, to a lower and more manageable order of
explanation. His effort as a *man* was to deal with them, find himself in relation to them in his own life. He was, if there ever was
one, a *pèlerin de l'absolu,* and only in considering him as such
can the paradoxes, struggles, failures, and achievements of his
life be understood.[6]

In the vast and varied literature concerning Coleridge's "case,"
as Richards calls it, there are many discussions which touch in
one way or another upon a central problem—the problem of the
part played by Coleridge's religious consciousness and needs in
determining the course of his poetic career—or, conversely, the
role that poetry, the poetic experience, played in Coleridge's
quest for the absolute.

Aside from the biographies,[7] the most extensive treatment of
the development of Coleridge's thought is that of J. H. Muirhead
in his book *Coleridge as Philosopher*[8] and in a subsequent article.[9] As the title of his book indicates, Muirhead is primarily

[6] See Sara Coleridge's Introduction to the *Biographia Literaria* (quoted by
Armour and Howes, *Coleridge the Talker* [Ithaca: Cornell University Press, 1940],
p. 29), in which she characterizes Coleridge as "one whose genius was ever impelling him to trace things down to their deepest sources, and follow them out to
their remotest ramifications." See also H. N. Coleridge's Preface to the second
edition of *The Table Talk* (also quoted by Armour and Howes, p. 148): "He
was, indeed, to my observation, more distinguished from other great men of letters by his moral thirst after Truth—the ideal truth—in his own mind, than by
his merely intellectual qualifications."

[7] J. D. Campbell, *Samuel Taylor Coleridge, a Narrative of the Events in His
Life* (London & New York: Macmillan, 1894); and Lawrence Hanson, *The Life
of Samuel Taylor Coleridge, the Early Years* (London: G. Allen & Unwin, 1938),
are the most extensive and dependable biographical studies.

[8] London: Macmillan, 1930.

[9] "Metaphysician or Mystic," *Coleridge, Studies by Several Hands on the Hundredth Anniversary of his Death,* ed. by Edmund Blunden and Earl Leslie Griggs
(London: Constable & Co. Ltd., 1934), pp. 179-97.

interested in tracing the doctrinal variations in Coleridge's thought rather than the history of his personal spiritual struggles. Although he is quite conscious of the central importance of personal religious experience in Coleridge's life,[10] Muirhead, a philosopher himself, is inclined to be impatient with Coleridge's religious preoccupation as a deterrent to philosophical clarity.[11] He is not, in any case, concerned with the relation between Coleridge's religious needs and his poetic career.

The same thing may be said of other less exhaustive earlier discussions such as those of Stopford Brooke,[12] John Tulloch,[13] V. F. Stoor,[14] and Herbert Stewart,[15] all of which are concerned in one way or another with the development of Coleridge's theological opinions, the influences those opinions were subject to, their relative orthodoxy, and their significance in the history of English theology. S. F. Gingerich, in his essay "From Necessity to Transcendentalism in Coleridge,"[16] makes the point that Coleridge's outlook on life was always essentially religious; but in discussing the reasons for Coleridge's poetic difficulties he looks to various circumstantial factors—illness, opium, lack of

[10] See *Coleridge as Philosopher*, p. 35, where Muirhead points out that Coleridge had a profoundly religious nature, not only in the Platonic or Spinozistic sense, "but in the sense of a longing for a personal relation with a Mind and Will as at once the source of all reality and a living presence in the soul." The burden of his article is that Coleridge was *not* a mystic in the sense of turning his back upon Reason or emancipating reason from its continuity with understanding, that for Coleridge the "Intuition" of Reason is a completion of thought.

[11] *Coleridge as Philosopher*, pp. 115-16.

[12] *Theology in the English Poets* (London: J. M. Dent & Sons, 1874), pp. 55-74.

[13] *Movements of Religious Thought in Britain in the Nineteenth Century* (London: Longmans, 1885).

[14] *Development of English Theology in the Nineteenth Century, 1800-1860* (London, New York: Longmans, Green, 1913).

[15] "The Place of Coleridge in English Theology," *Harvard Theological Review*, XVIII (1918).

[16] *PMLA*, XXXV (1920), 1-59, reprinted as a chapter in *Essays in the Romantic Poets* (New York: Macmillan, 1924), pp. 17-87.

domestic affection—and does not consider the possibility that the poetic crisis in Coleridge's life was in some way a religious crisis. He is interested in "Dejection" primarily as an indication of what he feels is Coleridge's conversion from determinism to transcendentalism.

Professor H. N. Fairchild's treatment of Coleridge in the third volume of his work *Religious Trends in English Poetry*[17] comes as a genuine disappointment, in view of the level of scholarship of the book as a whole and the perspective afforded by so extended a survey of religion in relation to poetry. The difficulty is that Fairchild appears to dislike and disapprove of Coleridge so intensely that the ultimate problems do not really arise for him. Departing from an entry in one of Coleridge's notebooks in which Coleridge says he had "been always preyed upon by some dread,"[18] he interprets Coleridge's whole life, as lover, poet, philosopher, and theologian, in terms of a flight from reality. Now, there is certainly an element of truth in this formulation, although taken as a general leitmotif it represents a vast oversimplification. But it *suggests* questions; it does not answer them. It may be true, as Fairchild exclaims concerning a letter of consolation that Coleridge wrote to Lamb, that Lamb was "a man who had more grace in his little finger than Coleridge was ever to possess!"[19] But, aside from the difficulty of measuring the presence of grace, this is again a beginning for enquiry, not grounds for dismissing it. Fairchild accepts Miss Schneider's argument that opium cannot be held responsible for the form or content of such poems as "Kubla Khan," but turns her evidence toward this puzzling conclusion:

[17] New York: Columbia University Press, 1949, pp. 263-327.
[18] *Inquiring Spirit*, ed. by Kathleen Coburn (London: Routledge and Paul, 1951), p. 54. See in this book p. 49.
[19] *Religious Trends*, p. 284.

Coleridge did not write poems like *Kubla Khan* because he was a drug-addict: he was a drug-addict because he was the sort of person who writes poems like *Kubla Khan*.[20]

Yet subsequently he attributes Coleridge's brief period of poetic success to "the joy of Wordsworth and the peace of laudanum."[21] If we accept these conclusions, serious questioning about the relation of religious and poetic experience in Coleridge's life is irrelevant. There is a profound sense in which Coleridge's life *is* a scandal, but nothing is to be gained in being scandalized by it. Much is to be gained by seeking the roots of that scandal in ultimate human terms. To do so is to understand what people have meant by calling Coleridge a "great failure."

As a preparation for his treatment of the problems surrounding Coleridge's "Hymn before Sunrise," Professor Adrien Bonjour offers an extended and very serious consideration of what he calls the "Dejection crisis."[22] In weighing the relative importance of various possible contributing causes, he follows Muirhead in maintaining that indulgence in metaphysics was less significant than Coleridge's own statements might lead us to believe. He lays greatest stress upon ill-health and opium, which he feels were responsible for inducing a decline of willpower that rendered Coleridge incapable of overcoming the inhibiting effect of any sense of obligation. There is no explicit consideration of the possible relation between Coleridge's religious evolution and his difficulties as a poet.

It is interesting that the most penetrating discussion of the importance of religious experience in Coleridge's life, and specifically in relation to his poetry, comes to us from Germany. Speaking of religion, Dr. Elizabeth Winkelmann says:

[20] *Ibid.*, p. 291.
[21] *Ibid.*, p. 292.
[22] *Coleridge's "Hymn before Sunrise", a Study of Facts and Problems Connected with the Poem* (Lausanne: Imprimerie La Concorde, 1942), Chap. I.

If we start out with this as the basic element, we find ourselves possessed of the real key to a deeper understanding of Coleridge's entire work. What in the last analysis is a purely religious motive, a longing for the supernatural, a striving to find a connection of some kind between the finite and the infinite, runs all through his work.[23]

This is surely a more plausible formulation than that of D. G. James, for instance, who, in terms similar to those of Fairchild, sees the *Grundmotiv* in Coleridge's life as a basic insecurity of mind, a "desire to retreat from the world and himself."[24] Miss Winkelmann, on the contrary, sees the various aspects of Coleridge's work as having a common religious motive:

However detached philosophy may have become from poetry in his career, still "to write poetry" and "to think" were not for him separate things but closely related, as two means of formulating his inner religious life.[25]

Another German commentator, Dr. Josephine Nettesheim, comes even closer than Miss Winkelmann not only to the realization of the central importance of religion in Coleridge's life but also to fixing the cause of his poetic crisis in these terms. She maintains that

For Coleridge the activity involved in writing poetry was neither a matter of verse-making nor a purely artistic experience, but rather a positive kind of religious experience. When he bemoans his diminishing "poetic production," he means that this kind of religious experience no longer affords him religious satisfaction.[26]

She places Coleridge in the line of Rousseau, Hamann, Herder, and Novalis, and interprets "Ode on the Departing Year,"

[23] *Coleridge und die Kantische Philosophie* (Leipzig: Mayer & Müller, 1933), p. 12.
[24] *The Romantic Comedy* (London: Oxford University Press, 1948), pp. 155 ff.
[25] *Coleridge und die Kantische Philosophie*, p. 13.
[26] "Das Erlöschen von Coleridge's 'dichterischer Produktion' um 1800," *Archiv für das Studium der neueren Sprachen und Literaturen*, CXLVI (1923), 214.

The Ancient Mariner, and "Kubla Khan" as having their source in religious-mystical experiences, and Coleridge's poetic production in general as *"mystisches Experimentieren."* The crisis occurs when it becomes evident that this last experiment in self-salvation, like enthusiasm for the French Revolution and for Pantisocracy, has failed; and so the way is left open for a reconversion to Christianity.[27]

My conclusions in this book will not differ greatly from those of Miss Nettesheim. I shall attempt to adjust certain emphases, to anticipate some objections, and, perhaps most important, to examine in some detail the peculiar relations between poetry and religious experience which permit and may even foster a confusion between the two, a confusion which can dry up the sources of the poetic experience without substantially nourishing the religious life. In order to clear the ground for an examination of the peculiarities of Coleridge's poetic career, and its significance for him as a person, it will first be necessary to consider two other aspects of his activity which have some bearing on his course as a poet: his preoccupation with philosophy and theology, and the emotional attachments in his life. Indeed, it has very frequently been suggested, even by Coleridge himself, that the vicissitudes of his poetic career are directly traceable to these factors as causes.[28] Although their causal significance may be doubtful, the examination of these elements in Coleridge's experience furnishes some illuminating suggestions with which to begin the consideration of his poetic experience. This consideration will take the form of a detailed analysis of the poem "Dejec-

---

[27] *Ibid.,* pp. 217-22.

[28] A third factor, to which Coleridge's failures and even some of his successes have even more often been attributed, is his addiction to opium. This will not be considered here, since the subject has recently been treated in a very thorough and conclusive manner by Miss Elisabeth Schneider in *Coleridge, Opium and "Kubla Khan"* (Chicago: University of Chicago Press, 1953).

tion: An Ode," showing first of all how its symbolism pervades Coleridge's whole poetic opus, then attempting to interpret the poem as an artistic record of the major crisis in Coleridge's poetic life. Finally, an effort will be made to translate the data of this personal experience of Coleridge's into some more general aesthetic terms and suggest what its significance may be in relation to the historical development of poetry.

In doing this, special attention will be paid to the relation between Coleridge's experience and that of certain continental Romantics. Students of comparative literature have by this time explored rather extensively some of the relations between British and continental Romantics, but their studies, especially those concerned with Coleridge, have for the most part dealt with "influences." And in an age characterized by a new emphasis on the exploration of the individual psyche, literary influences are probably less important than they are in many other periods. In the effort to understand the Romantic period, it is most important to note more or less isolated growths of a similar character. Individuals who in juxtaposition with their immediate compatriots seem almost pathologically eccentric tend to emerge as quite normal precursors of an age to follow when they are seen in the company of peers who were perhaps completely unknown to them. And so, although it might make Coleridge himself rather uncomfortable, there is some justification in trying to shift our image of him a little away from Lamb, Southey, and Wordsworth and a little closer to Moritz, Novalis, Baudelaire, and Rimbaud.

I

POETRY VERSUS
"ABSTRUSE RESEARCHES"

The various commentators on Coleridge's "failure" may be divided roughly into two groups: those who see it primarily as the result of conflict between his different intellectual activities and those who place the principal blame on misfortunes, flaws of character, and physical ailments. Among the first group are those who, guided perhaps by their own interests in approaching Coleridge, begin with the assumption that he was essentially a poet, and conclude that his poetic gifts were either spoiled or wasted as a result of his preoccupation with metaphysics and theology, or, more generally, as a result of his tendency towards abstraction. John Wilson, writing in *Blackwood's Magazine* in 1840, put it well and briefly: "He wrote good poetry in his youth; but muddled his Helicon with metaphysics as he fell into years."[1] Robert Percival Graves, in a letter to a friend soon after Coleridge's death, reports that

Wordsworth, as a poet, regretted that German metaphysics had so much captivated the taste of Coleridge, for he was frequently not intelligible on this subject; whereas, if his energy and his originality had been more exerted in the channel of poetry, an instrument of which he had so perfect a mastery, Wordsworth thought he might have done

[1] "The Late James Smith," *Blackwood's Magazine*, XLVIII (September, 1840), 364-65, quoted by Armour and Howes, *Coleridge the Talker*, p. 370.

more permanently to enrich literature, and so to influence the thought of the nation, than any man of his age.[2]

This assumption that Coleridge was essentially a poet side-tracked by metaphysics is not unreasonable, in view of several facts. He is certainly best known as a poet, a fact which indicates posterity's judgment that his achievements as a poet are superior to his achievements in any of the other fields he entered. And at his poetic best he is so good that one is tempted, like Wordsworth, to be impatient with him for letting himself stray from what was undoubtedly a real vocation for him. Finally, it is true that this conflict between the claims of poetry and the more "abstract" pursuits furnished matter of doubt, contradiction, and painful introspection for Coleridge himself. In 1800, comparing himself to Wordsworth, he said, "As to our literary occupations they are still more distant than our residences—He is a great, a true Poet—I am only a kind of Metaphysician."[3] In 1802 he said that although sickness and worse afflictions had forced him into downright metaphysics, "I believe that by nature I have more of the poet in me."[4] In the same month he wrote:

As to myself, all my poetic genius (if ever I really possessed any *genius,* and it was not rather a mere general *aptitude* of talent, and quickness in imitation) is gone, and I have been fool enough to suffer deeply in my mind, regretting the loss, which I attribute to my long and exceedingly severe metaphysical investigations, and these partly to ill-health, and partly to private afflictions which rendered any subjects immediately concerned with feeling, a source of pain and disquiet to me.[5]

---

[2] Quoted by Armour and Howes, *Coleridge the Talker,* p. 378.

[3] *Unpublished Letters,* ed. by Earl Leslie Griggs (London: Constable & Co. Ltd., 1932), I, 165 (to the Rev. F. Wrangham, December 19, 1800).

[4] *Letters of Samuel Taylor Coleridge,* ed. by E. H. Coleridge (Boston and New York: Houghton, Mifflin, 1895), I, 378 (to W. Sotheby, July 19, 1802).

[5] *Ibid.,* p. 388 (to Southey, July 29, 1802).

In *The Friend* (1809-10), he said that

long and early habits of exerting my intellect in metrical composition have not so enslaved me, but that for some years I have felt, and deeply felt, that the poet's high functions were not my proper assignment; . . . I feel it as a blessing, that even among my contemporaries I know one at least, who has been deemed worthy of the gift; who has received the harp with reverence, and struck it with the hand of power.[6]

Another comparison of himself with Wordsworth. In 1818 he said that "Poetry is out of the question," because he lacked "competence" and "joyous circumstances," and he bemoaned the fact, by now with resignation—"But God's will be done."[7]

In view of Coleridge's own uncertainty and even contradiction concerning the matter, it might be well to begin with a critical examination of this way of posing the problem, beginning with the assumption that "Coleridge was a poet." Now, there are certainly various intelligible and useful senses in which the locution "X is a poet" is employed, e.g.:

X is sensitive to things in a way that one thinks should enable him to write poetry.

X's makeup, both as a result of his natural tendencies and of the influences to which he has been subjected, is such that any attempts he makes to embody or develop the experiences which this sensitivity occasions are more likely to be made through the medium of poetic composition than, say, painting or musical composition.

X in fact writes poetry.

X's poems are his most outstanding or valuable product.

X's principal work is the writing of poetry.

---

[6] *Complete Works*, ed. by W. G. T. Shedd (New York: Harper, 1853), II, 533.
[7] *Letters*, II, 694 (to W. Collins, December, 1818).

Difficulties might arise over such terms as "sensitive," "makeup," or "natural tendencies," and the truth of many such statements may be difficult to establish in the case of a given person; but concerning each of these senses of the expression there would seem to be ways of establishing the probable truth, at least of agreeing or disagreeing about it intelligibly.

But the expression "X is a poet" is also used in a quite different way, which makes of it a statement of a quite different order, a statement whose truth or falsehood cannot be established, or even intelligibly disagreed about, because it is a nonsense. I refer to the use of the expression which makes of it a kind of ultimate ontological statement, as when we say that "X is a poet" in a way that is analogous to saying "X is right-handed" or "X is male." This is probably sometimes the sense of the statement "X is a *born* poet," meaning that being a poet is something inscribed in his very being at its origin.[8] Coleridge is perhaps using the expression with something of this force when he compares Cowper to Thomson in the *Biographia Literaria.* Cowper qualified as a poet, and, in ways important to Coleridge, a good one: he "combined natural thoughts with natural diction"; he "reconciled the heart with the head"; his *Task* was an "excellent poem"; and "in chastity of diction . . . and the harmony of blank verse, Cowper leaves Thomson immeasurably below him." "Yet," said Coleridge, and the italics are his, "still I feel the latter to have been the *born* poet."[9]

A good deal of discussion of Coleridge and his difficulties, including some of Coleridge's own discussion thereof, seems to be

---

[8] This sense of being a poet might be intelligible if it were applied to all men, to mean that the poetic experience is a generic human experience, growing out of the very nature of man's consciousness and its ways of apprehending reality—one of which is what St. Thomas Aquinas and Coleridge call knowledge by connaturality—but this would be a different matter.

[9] Ed. by J. Shawcross (London: Oxford University Press, 1939), I, 16.

a debate as to whether the statement "Coleridge was a poet," employed in this latter way, is true or not. If one takes the affirmative in this debate, then one will be inclined to judge Coleridge's attempts to "be" anything other than a poet (to be, for instance, a metaphysician, a theologian, or a politician) in any serious, time-consuming manner, in something like the same way one might judge a male's attempt to be a female—at best unfortunate and misguided, at worst even downright perverted. One would be led to inquire what sent him off on this unnatural tangent: we have seen that when Coleridge is taking this view of the matter, he offers sickness and afflictions as the immediate cause. If one employs the expression "X is a poet" in this way, one conceives that being a poet is what is "natural," "right" for X, and that deviations from this line are somehow or other "sick." And in these terms, failure in other fields as well is explained (Coleridge was never successful as a philosopher because he was really a poet—women make much better women than people who are really men).

But if the expression "X is a born poet" is really meaningful only as a kind of metaphor, if no intelligible or verifiable literal meaning can be assigned to it, then to confound this metaphorical use with the various intelligible and verifiable literal uses of the expression in one's practical thinking and reflection about one's own career could give rise to serious confusions and needless anguish. To confound them in one's analysis of someone else's career would certainly give rise to serious misinterpretations and complex disputes over pseudo-problems.

Coleridge's most comprehensive statement of this view of his career occurs in the *Biographia Literaria*. The statement is as follows:

At a very premature age, even before my fifteenth year, I had bewildered myself in metaphysicks, and in theological controversy.

Nothing else pleased me. History, and particular facts, lost all interest in my mind. Poetry (though for a school-boy of that age, I was
above par in English versification, and had already produced two or
three compositions which, I may venture to say, without reference to
my age, were somewhat above mediocrity, and which gained me
more credit than the sound, good sense of my old master was at all
pleased with,) poetry itself, yea, novels and romances, became insipid
to me. In my friendless wanderings on our leave-days (for I was an
orphan, and had scarcely any connections in London,) highly was I
delighted, if any passenger, especially if he were drest in black, would
enter into conversation with me. For I soon found the means of di-
recting it to my favorite subjects

'Of providence, fore-knowledge, will, and fate,
Fix'd fate, free will, fore-knowledge absolute,
And found no end in wandering mazes lost.'

This preposterous pursuit was, beyond doubt, injurious both to my
natural powers, and to the progress of my education. It would perhaps have been destructive, had it been continued; but from this I
was auspiciously withdrawn, partly indeed by an accidental introduction to an amiable family, chiefly however, by the genial influence
of a style of poetry, so tender and yet so manly, so natural and real,
and yet so dignified and harmonious, as the sonnets &c. of Mr.
Bowles! Well were it for me, perhaps, had I never relapsed into the
same mental disease; if I had continued to pluck the flower and reap
the harvest from the cultivated surface, instead of delving in the unwholesome quick-silver mines of metaphysic depths. But if in after
time I sought a refuge from bodily pain and mismanaged sensibility
in abstruse researches, which exercised the strength and subtlety of
the understanding without awakening the feelings of the heart; still
there was a long and blessed interval, during which my natural
faculties were allowed to expand, and my original tendencies to de-
velope themselves; my fancy, and the love of nature, and the sense
of beauty in forms and sounds.[10]

[10] I, 9-10.

The role assigned by Coleridge to his emotional afflictions will be considered later. For the moment we may take at face value what he says here about his second attack of metaphysics being brought on by such causes. But the first attack, at so early an age, was clearly not so motivated: he first indulged in metaphysics and theological controversy because it "pleased" him to do so, fascinated him even more than writing poetry, in which he was already reasonably proficient. The fact is, as he indicated a few pages earlier, that some of his early poetry, even some written during the happy intermission he speaks of here, was motivated by these very metaphysical interests.[11] In short, this effort on Coleridge's part to classify his interests and to separate his life into neatly distinct periods according to their ascendancy cannot be taken as a satisfactory account of the facts, any more than his characterization of his poetic faculties as the "natural" ones and his philosophical activities as a "disease," especially since Coleridge himself both before and after took contrary views. In 1803 he asked,

What is it that I employ my metaphysics on, To perplex our clearest notions and living moral instincts? To extinguish the light of love and of conscience, to put out the life of arbitrement, to make myself and others *worthless, soulless, Godless?* No, to expose the folly and the legerdemain of those who have thus abused the blessed organ of language, to support all old and venerable truths, to support, to kindle, to project, to make the reason spread light over our feelings, to make our feelings diffuse vital warmth through our reason—these are my objects and these my subjects. Is this the metaphysic that bad spirits in hell delight in?[12]

And, we may ask, is this a "mental disease"? It is important to recall that in the passage previously cited (p. 16) he listed as one

[11] *Ibid.*, p. 3.
[12] *Anima Poetae,* ed. by E. H. Coleridge (London: Wm. Heinemann, 1895), pp. 42-43.

of Cowper's qualifications as a *poet* the fact that he "reconciled the heart with the head," and that later on he said of the mystics Fox, Behmen, and Law that "they contributed to keep alive the *heart* in the *head*."[13] And so we have poetry, metaphysics, and the mystical experience all referred to as contributing to the same end—an integration of the human being, in harmony with the universe in which he finds himself. In another work of the same period he said that "no man was ever a great poet, without being at the same time a profound philosopher."[14] And in the last year of his life he said of himself, "I am by the law of my nature a reasoner."[15] If we took some of these statements as definitive, we should be led to the conclusion that Coleridge was "really" a philosopher, and that it is too bad he wasted so much time and energy on poetry to the detriment of his philosophical development.

Also suspect, and illuminating, is his contrast between poetry as plucking the flower and reaping the harvest from the cultivated surface and philosophical activity as "delving in the unwholesome quicksilver mines of metaphysic depths." It would be difficult to think in what sense it was "natural" or "original" with Coleridge to content himself with plucking from the surface. As he himself indicates, his poetic activity itself was just the contrary of that. Surely it was the delving that was "natural," whether philosophic or poetic. As a matter of fact, Coleridge used this same metaphor on another occasion in the reverse direction. He wrote in one of his notebooks that "Abstruse reasoning is to the inductions of common sense what reaping is to delving. But the implements with which we reap, how are

13 *Biographia Literaria*, I, 98.
14 *A Lay Sermon*, in *Complete Works*, VI, 499.
15 *Specimens of the Table Talk of Samuel Taylor Coleridge*, ed. by H. N. Coleridge (London: John Murray, 1851), p. 308.

they gained? by delving."[16] In the *Biographia Literaria* he distinguishes between Wordsworth's object in writing the Preface to *Lyrical Ballads* and his own object in the *Biographia* by saying that

it was Mr. Wordsworth's purpose to consider the influence of fancy and imagination as they are manifested in poetry, and from the different effects to conclude their diversity in kind; while it is my object to investigate the seminal principle, and then from the kind to deduce the degree. My friend has drawn a masterly sketch of the branches with their *poetic* fruitage. I wish to add the trunk, and even the roots as far as they lift themselves above the ground, and are visible to the naked eye of our common consciousness.[17]

The "long and blessed interval" during which he remembers himself to have been free of the disease of metaphysics can hardly have lasted more than six years, from the time he met the Evans family in 1788, at the age of sixteen, until 1794, when we find him writing to Southey, "I am so habituated to philosophizing that I cannot divest myself of it; even when my own wretchedness is the subject."[18] And, most important to note, it ended *before* the composition of his greatest poems. In 1795 he was delivering lectures in Bristol on theological and political subjects, and in 1796, still prior to the composition of poems like *The Ancient Mariner* and *Christabel,* he wrote to Thelwall:

I am *deep* in all out of the way books, whether of the monkish times, or of the puritanical era. I have read and digested most of the historical writings; but I do not *like* history. Metaphysics and poetry and 'facts of mind', that is, accounts of all the strange phantasms that ever possessed 'your philosophy'; . . . I compose very little, and I absolutely hate composition, and such is my dislike that even a sense of duty is sometimes too weak to overpower it.[19]

[16] *Anima Poetae,* p. 51, between items dated 1803.
[17] I, 64.
[18] *Letters,* I, 106.
[19] *Ibid.,* p. 181.

From other letters we know that he was reading Kant, the neo-Platonists, and Hartley. In 1797, at the peak of his poetic activity, he was reading Berkeley and Spinoza. In 1798 he embarked on a short preaching career, from which he was rescued by a subsidy from the Wedgwood brothers, for the purpose of working on what was to be his philosophical *magnum opus* (which was never realized in fact but on which he said, in 1821, that he had spent three fourths of his intellectual life[20]). In the same year (1798) he departed for Germany to pursue his philosophical studies. In 1799, back in England, he said he was "sunk in Spinoza."[21]

In view of the apparent contradictions in Coleridge's own statements about the relation between his career as a poet and his philosophical pursuits, it would be well to review briefly the indisputable facts in the case to see what actually happened in terms of time spent and production. The facts are these, relative to his "poetic" career:

Coleridge lived for sixty-two years.

He wrote poetry at least as early as the age of fifteen (1787).

He wrote some poems every year from the age of fifteen through that of thirty-three (1805).

His most prolific activity occurred in the six-year period between the ages of twenty-two and twenty-eight (1794 to 1800).

All of his long poems were written within this six-year period.

All of his recognizedly "great" poems were written within this same period, the most generally admired within two years, 1797-98.

From the age of thirty-three until his death, a period of twenty-

---

[20] *Letters, Conversations, and Recollections of Samuel Taylor Coleridge,* ed. by Thomas Alsop (London: Frederick Farrah, 1864), p. 83.

[21] *Unpublished Letters,* I, 126 (to Robert Southey, September 30, 1799).

nine years, he wrote some complete poems during every year, with the exception of seven (1816, 1818, 1819, 1821, 1822, 1831, and the year of his death, 1834).

After 1802 there are a good many whole years represented by only one, two, or three short poems. For example, the year 1804 is represented by only two four-line stanzas of which one is:

> We pledged our hearts, my love and I,—
>   I in my arms the maiden clasping;
> I could not guess the reason why,
>   But, oh! I trembled like an aspen.[22]

On the side of his "abstract" pursuits, the facts seem to be the following:

His earliest preoccupation with philosophy and theology was contemporaneous with his earliest poetic compositions.

If there was an interruption in this preoccupation, it occurred between 1788 and 1794, a period not characterized by the production of a great deal of poetry or of poetry of particularly high quality.

His philosophical activities continued through the period of greatest poetic production, 1794-99, and included his first contact with Kant, one of the important philosophical influences in his life.

The latter half of his life was almost exclusively devoted to "abstruse researches"—philosophical, theological, critical, political.

The "explanation" with which we have been dealing here can be summarized as involving the following propositions: (1) that one is "born" a poet in something like the same way one is born a male, and that Coleridge was so born; (2) that in spite of this fact, and for various extraneous reasons, Coleridge became pre-

[22] *The Poems of Samuel Taylor Coleridge,* ed. by E. H. Coleridge (London: Oxford University Press, 1945), p. 391. This work will subsequently be referred to simply as *Poems.*

occupied with metaphysics; (3) that this preoccupation was responsible for his ceasing to produce poetry of the calibre he was capable of producing, because the two activities, metaphysical research and writing poetry, are naturally and inevitably conflicting as activities of one and the same person. In short, Coleridge did not continue as a great poet because he "became" a metaphysician. As we have seen, Coleridge himself at times seems to take this position concerning himself.

I have suggested that the first of these propositions is either a metaphorical statement or, if taken literally, a nonsense. But even if we should leave this out of account, the facts outlined here, reinforced by some of Coleridge's own statements and by what is evident from reading his poetic works, seem in the first place to offer conclusive evidence that Coleridge *was* a poet in most of the literal and verifiable senses of that expression, throughout his life. They also suggest, again taking into consideration some of his own statements and the quality of his best poems, that something "happened" to him as a poet, and that it happened sometime around 1802. But it is equally clear that the formula he sometimes offers as an explanation, aside from being based in part on a concealed metaphor, does not stand up in the face of these facts. Whatever the relation between his poetical and his philosophical activities, the latter cannot be said to have intervened at some point and blighted his poetic gifts. If he was a poet from the first it must equally be said that he was a philosopher from the first. The fact that after a certain point in his life his deep inner experiences and insights no longer issued in poetic creation cannot be laid to his taking up metaphysics (for whatever reason he did so), and so remains to be accounted for. Something "muddled his Helicon," but it was not the introduction of metaphysics.

II

LOVE AND THE POETIC EXPERIENCE

Some critics have suggested that Coleridge's difficulties and disappointments in love are the most important key to understanding the vicissitudes of his poetic career.[1] They point out that his *annus mirabilis* roughly coincided with the brief period of his happiness in marriage (reinforced by the intellectual companionship of the Wordsworths in the first bloom of their friendship), and that when this environment of love and contentment was shattered, his productiveness ceased. Although he knew love subsequently, it was unfulfilled, and a source of agony rather than of happiness. This explanation seems not unlikely in the nature of things, and further, we have numerous statements by Coleridge linking his unproductiveness to "private afflictions," and expressing most poignantly his need for love.

Some examination of the facts in the case, and of Coleridge's statements about them, may aid in bringing the importance of love in Coleridge's personality and experience into perspective, and in showing its relation to other elements. For instance, it may be that Coleridge's experiences in love explain in part his acute religious consciousness—or perhaps the explanation might better

---

[1] See, for instance, G. Wilson Knight, *The Starlit Dome* (London: Oxford University Press, 1943), p. 101, and Adrien Bonjour, *Coleridge's "Hymn before Sunrise,"* pp. 62ff. See also Coleridge's letter to John S. Morgan, March 17, 1808, *Unpublished Letters,* I, 403.

go in the other direction; that is, his acute religious consciousness may have been at the root of his life-long need for love, in
the almost metaphysical form which that need took with him.
Coleridge made the connection himself when he cited the fact
that marriage is "chosen by St. Paul as the symbol of the union
of the church with Christ: that is, of the souls of all good men
with God."[2]

But in Coleridge's own experience the relation between human
love and mystical union with God seems to have been more than
symbolic. He seems to have sought in human love the satisfaction
of a specifically religious need. The clearest expressions of this
occur in his notebooks, at the height of his attachment to Sara
Hutchinson between 1805 and 1810. Of his terrible need for love
he said,

> I am so feeble that I cannot yearn to be perfect, unrewarded by some
> distinct goal, yet still somewhat too noble to be satisfied, or even
> pleased, by the assent of the many. Myself will not suffice, and a
> stranger is nothing. It must be one who is, and who is not my-
> self. . . .[3]

This doubtless goes no further than most introspective lovers
would go, but there is more:

> For love, passionate in its deepest tranquility, love unutterable, fills
> my whole spirit—so that every fibre of my heart, nay, of my whole
> frame, seems to tremble under its perpetual touch and sweet pressure,
> like the string of a lute—with a sense of vibrating pain, a pain that
> seems to shiver and tremble on the threshold of some joy which
> cannot be entered into while I am embodied—a pain of yearning
> which all the pleasure on earth could not enduce me to relinquish,
> even were it in my power; and yet it *is* a pain, an aching, that

[2] *Notes, Theological, Political, and Miscellaneous*, ed. by Derwent Coleridge
(London: Edward Moxon, 1853), p. 272.

[3] Cited in T. M. Raysor, "Coleridge and Asra," *Studies in Philology*, XXVI
(1929), 314. Cf. *Unpublished Letters*, II, 44-49 (to Crabb Robinson, March, 1811).

spreads even into the eyes, that have a look as if they were asking a what and a where even of vacancy—yea, even when the Beloved is present seeming to look through her and asking for her very self within and even beyond her apparent form.[4]

Coleridge is obviously trying here to describe a state of mind as sensitively and accurately as he can, and he is an unusually sensitive and accurate observer. He feels himself approaching a joy which cannot be entered into while he is embodied, asking for a fulfillment which lies beyond the presence, the apparent form of the Beloved. In fact, what he is asking for here corresponds to a state beyond that of the mystical union with God, that obscure knowledge through experienced contact which the mystics tell of and which is, after all, experienced in the bodily state, and in this life. Coleridge is longing, it would seem, for something like the beatific vision, a complete presence and union in full knowledge, which according to mystical theology takes place only in the afterlife.

In the passage which follows, written two years later, in 1810, he is using language concerning his love for "Asra" which is even more explicitly appropriate to the mystical love of God. We should find nothing at all unusual if we read, "My love of God is not so much in my soul, as my soul in it." One hears an echo of St. Paul. What Coleridge says is:

My love of ,Kθγ is not so much in my soul, as my soul in it. It is my whole being wrapt into one desire, all the hopes and fears, joys and sorrows, all the powers, vigor, and faculties of my spirit abridged into one perpetual inclination. To bid me not to love you were to bid me to annihilate myself, for to love you is all I know of my life as far as my life is an object of my consciousness or my free will.

---

[4] Raysor, "Coleridge and Asra," p. 318 (entry of September 9, 1808). An interesting comparison can be made in this connection between Coleridge and Poe. Cf. Allen Tate, "Our Cousin, Mr. Poe," *The Forlorn Demon* (Chicago: Regnery, 1953), pp. 79-95.

And it turns out that he is himself conscious that he is treading
on dangerous ground, for he continues:

God is our being, but thro' his works alone doth he reveal himself—
and that for which all other objects have a vital meaning, possess
either force or attraction, are desired or avoided—that of which all
other objects are a copious language of epithets and synonyms—that
is God appearing to me, in that he reveals himself, and in that I love
and adore him. I hold it, therefore, neither impiety on the one hand
nor superstition on the other that you are the God within me, even
as the best and most religious men have called their conscience the
God within them. But you, tho' existing to my senses, have ever
abode within me. You have been, and you alone have been my conscience—in what form, with what voice, under what modifications,
can I imagine God to work on me, in which *you* have not worked?
All evil has kept aloof—you have worked ceaselessly, everywhere, at
all times, and the sum of your influence and benignant grace has been
horror of whatever is base, shame and compunction for whatever is
weak and unworthy, fervent aspirations after good and great and
honorable and beautiful things, and the unconquerable necessity of
making myself worthy of being happy as the one indispensable condition of possessing the one only happiness, your love, your esteem,
and *you*.[5]

It should be emphasized that these passages are not from love
letters, not written to impress his beloved and so characterized
by the exaggeration natural in expressions of that kind. They occur in Coleridge's private notebooks, and are to be taken as con-
scientious efforts to analyze his feelings. Nor are they the result
of the first impact of a new love—Coleridge met and fell in love
with Sara Hutchinson in 1799. And they are even cautious statements: "to love you is all I know of my life . . . as far as my life
is an object of my consciousness or my free will."

A poetic treatment of the quality of love, written some years
earlier than these notebook entries, deserves attention in this con-

[5] Raysor, "Coleridge and Asra," p. 319 (entry of October 24, 1810).

nection. In the fall of 1800 Coleridge began and left unfinished "a sort of dramatic romance" called *The Triumph of Loyalty,* in which the hero describes thus the moment of his declaration of love:

> I have small memory of aught but pleasure.
> The inquietudes of fear, like lesser Streams
> Still flowing, still were lost in those of love:
> So Love grew mightier from the Fear, and Nature,
> Fleeing from Pain, shelter'd herself in Joy.
> The stars above our heads were dim and steady,
> Like eyes suffus'd with rapture. Life was in us:
> We were all life, each atom of our Frames
> A living soul—I vow'd to die for her:
> With the faint voice of one who, having spoken,
> Relapses into blessedness, I vow'd it:
> That solemn Vow, a whisper scarcely heard
> A murmur breath'd against a lady's Cheek.
> Oh! there is Joy above the name of Pleasure,
> Deep self-possession, an intense Repose.
> No other than as Eastern Sages feign,
> The God, who floats upon a Lotos Leaf,
> Dreams for a thousand ages; then awaking,
> Creates a world, and smiling at the bubble,
> Relapses into bliss.[6]

In 1817 Coleridge published an excerpt from *The Triumph of Loyalty* as "The Night-Scene, a Dramatic Fragment," consisting of 83 lines, including the lines quoted above.[7] In this version the last five lines here quoted are placed in the mouth of the hero's interlocutor, who interrupts him "with a sarcastic smile." But in 1800 Coleridge was able without any irony or apology to compare the love experience to something even loftier than the beatific vision, to God's self-contemplation.

[6] *Poems,* p. 569.
[7] *Ibid.,* p. 422.

Another poetic expression relevant here is the little poem "Phantom," written probably in 1804 or 1805.

> All look and likeness caught from earth
> All accident of kin or birth,
> Had pass'd away. There was no trace
> Of aught on that illumined face,
> Uprais'd beneath the rifted stone
> But of one spirit all her own;—
> She, she herself, and only she,
> Shone through her body visibly.[8]

E. H. Coleridge points out that the lines occur in a notebook entry "to illustrate the idea that the love-sense can be abstracted from the accidents of form or person."[9] The poem is, in fact, very close in thought to something Coleridge discussed in one of the essays Cottle published as appendixes to his *Early Recollections:*

The safest definition then of BEAUTY, as well as the oldest, is that of Pythagoras: THE REDUCTION OF THE MANY TO ONE. . . .

The mystics meant the same, when they define beauty as a subjection of matter to spirit so as to be transformed into a symbol, in and through which the spirit reveals itself; and declare that the most beautiful, where the most obstacles to a full manifestation have been most perfectly overcome.

Coleridge then goes on to quote a passage from Plotinus:

'So with the perceptive faculty: discerning in certain objects the Ideal-Form which has bound and controlled [shapeless matter], opposed in nature to Idea, seeing farther stamped upon the common shapes some shape excellent above the common, it gathers into unity what still remains fragmentary, catches it up and carries it within, no

---

[8] *Ibid.,* p. 393.

[9] *Ibid.,* p. 393n. Coleridge might almost be saying with Baudelaire, "ce qu'il y a d'ennuyeux dans l'amour, c'est que c'est un crime où l'on ne peut pas se passer d'un complice." *Mon Coeur Mis à Nu,* in *Oeuvres Posthumes,* ed. by Eugène Crépit (Paris: Maison Quantin, 1887), p. 92.

longer a thing of parts, and presents it to the Ideal-Principle as something concordant and congenial, a natural friend.'[10]

A divine passage faintly represented in the following lines, written many years ago by the writer, though without reference to or recollection of the above.[11]

The lines which follow are lines 47-75 and 29-38 of "Dejection." "Dejection," in this light, is the account of the failure of the mystical experience of beauty; "Phantom" an account of a remembered momentary success, aided by the love-sense—but used to illustrate the idea that love can be abstracted from the accidents of form and person. E. H. Coleridge remarks that "both poems ['Phantom' and a related poem, 'Phantom or Fact'] are 'fragments from the life of dreams'; but it was the reality which lay behind both 'phantom' and 'fact' of which the poet dreamt, having his eyes open." On the contrary, Coleridge was probably using the lines quite aptly to illustrate his idea about love's being abstractable from accidents. The great fact of his love experiences is precisely that he had a way of looking right through "realities" toward something like "Reality"; and when he failed to attain it, the "realities" themselves became phantoms, even phantoms of the kind that excite fear.

A fragment, somewhat later in date, involves a kind of transfiguration:

[10] Coleridge quotes the passage in Greek. This translation is found in *The Ethical Treatises*, trans. by Stephen Mackenna (London and Boston: The Medici Society, 1926), I, 81. The Greek text (from *Plotini Opera*, ed. by Paul Henry and Hans-Rudolph Schwyzer, Paris, 1951, I, 107-8) follows:

Ὅταν οὖν καὶ ἡ αἴσθησις τὸ ἐν σώμασιν εἶδος ἴδῃ συνδησάμενον καὶ κρατῆσαν τῆς φύσεως τῆς ἐναντίας [ἀμόρφου οὔσης] καὶ μορφὴν ἐπ[ὶ] ἄλλαις μορφαῖς ἐκπρεπῶς ἐποχουμένην, συνελοῦσα ἀθρόον αὐτὸ τὸ πολλαχῇ ἀνήνεγκέ τε καὶ [εἰσήγαγεν εἰς τὸ εἴσω ἀμερὲς ἤδη καὶ] ἔδωκε τῷ ἔνδον σύμφωνον καὶ συναρμόττον καὶ φίλον· [bracketed material omitted by Coleridge].

[11](London: Longmans, 1837), II, 229-30; reprinted in *Biographia Literaria*, II, 238-39.

> The builder left one narrow rent,
>   Two wedded hearts, if ere were such,
> Contented most in discontent,
>   Still there cling, and try in vain to touch!
>
> O Joy! with thy own joy at strife,
>   That yearning for the Realm above
> Wouldst die into intenser Life,
>   And Union absolute of Love![12]

It is not that the properly mystical element noted here in Coleridge's feelings toward the woman he loved is unique or preternatural. More extreme statements ought not to be hard to find in the notebooks and letters of a wide variety of people. Its peculiar significance in the case of Coleridge can be appreciated only when it is taken together with what we know of his experience in other realms, and the fact that he was theologically sophisticated and self-conscious, and so not likely to fall into terminology of this kind as a simple metaphorical device. In order to assess that significance, it would be useful to examine evidence of his earlier experiences with love.

Although he speaks of having been spoiled as a child, there is little indication that he received much real affection, or affection based on any degree of understanding of the kind of creature he was. In addressing a poem to his brother George in 1797, he puts the most indulgent face on this deficiency in his childhood when he says that he was "too soon transplanted ere my soul had fix'd / Its first domestic loves."[13] His one close emotional attachment in

---

[12] *Poems*, pp. 500-1. There is another version of this fragment, which differs considerably in detail, and which lacks the last line. Compare with this fragment a statement of the German Romantic, Karl Gustave Carus (1789-1869), who, in speaking of the superiority of feeling, says that love, which is the highest form of feeling, is "the first deliverance from separate existence, the first step in the return to the All." Cited by Béguin, *L'Ame Romantique*, I, 252, from *Psyche, zur Entwicklungsgeschichte der Seele* (Pforzheim; Flammer and Hoffman, 1848), p. 297.

[13] *Poems*, p. 174; cf. also lines 39-42.

his family seems to have been to his sister, who died when he was nineteen. It was to her that he "pour'd forth all [his] puny sorrows . . . and of the heart those hidden maladies."[14] There is no suggestion then or later that his mother filled this void. His references to her in his letters are usually no more than dutifully correct. He seems sometimes almost to make a point of sending his "duty to our Mother" while sending expressions of affection even to his sisters-in-law. As early as 1788, long before his mother died, he sought motherly affection from Mrs. Evans, the mother of the girl who was his first love. In "Disappointment" he speaks of her and her daughter as "my parent and my friend."[15] In 1791 he says that quitting Christ's Hospital caused him "as great a pang" as when he was "torn by early sorrow [his father's death when he was nine years old] from my native seat."[16] Leaving the vicinity of the Evanses surely had a good deal to do with the sharpness of the pang.

Already in 1791 he knew what quality of love he sought in a woman, that quality which attracted him to the two women with whom he was in love in his life, and which was notably lacking in his wife: he wanted a lovely maid to read his visage in his mind.[17] The desire has seldom been expressed more succinctly. (If he was never in love with Dorothy Wordsworth, which itself is not certain, so imprecise is the term, it was perhaps that he found her not "lovely" enough—she seems to have been very good at reading his visage.) In "Genevieve," which belongs to the same period, he says he loves because of his beloved's capacity for understanding pity;[18] and he repeats the idea two years later in "The Hour When We Shall Meet Again."[19] In these days,

14 *Poems*, p. 78, "To a Friend," lines 13-15.
15 *Ibid.*, p. 34.
16 *Ibid.*, p. 29.
17 *Ibid.*, p. 32.
18 *Ibid.*, p. 20.
19 *Ibid.*, pp. 49, 96.

when he still had hope of fulfillment in love, and in poetry, he
sent to Mary Evans the lines:

> in discontent
> Restless thro' Fortune's mingled scenes I went,
> Yet wept to think they would return no more!
> O cease fond heart! in such sad thoughts to roam,
> For surely thou ere long shalt reach thy home,
> And pleasant is the way that lies before.[20]

Coleridge evidently tried with considerable good will to believe that he had found what he sought with Sara Fricker, though
he went to the marriage a very reluctant bridegroom, and never
quite forgave Southey for pressuring him into it.[21] It is hard not
to see a direct biographical reference in the opening lines of the
fragment *The Triumph of Loyalty* (the title itself would serve
as a description of Coleridge's marriage):

> *Sandoval.* You loved the daughter of Don Manrique?
> *Earl Henry.* Loved?
> *Sand.* Did you not say you wooed her?
> *Earl H.* Once I loved
> Her whom I dared not woo!
> *Sand.* And wooed perchance,
> One whom you loved not!
> *Earl H.* Oh! I were most base,
> Not loving Oropeza. True, I wooed her,
> Hoping to heal a deeper wound; but she

---

[20] *Ibid.*, pp. 56-57.
[21] Cf. Letter to John Morgan, March 17, 1808, *Unpublished Letters*, I, 403. In
her edition of the *Notebooks* (New York: Pantheon, 1957), Vol. II, note to entry
1815, 16.199, Kathleen Coburn cites evidence that Sara Fricker at first supposed
that Southey was attracted to her rather than to her sister Edith, whom he actually
married. This would furnish a more than Pantisocratic reason for Southey's zeal
in urging Coleridge to do his duty by Sara, and would relieve Coleridge of some
of his responsibility for the failure of the marriage in the sequel. In comparison
with Coleridge, Southey turned out to be a model husband; he was married to
Sara's own sister, and Sara had that happy pair under her eyes for long intervals.
The possibility for psychological complications, already rich, becomes overwhelming with the addition of this element.

> Met my advances with impassioned pride,
> That kindled love with love.[22]

Coleridge had not dared to woo Mary Evans, until it was too late; and he did woo Sara Fricker, hoping, precisely, to heal that deeper wound. In his effort to convince himself that he had succeeded, he dwelt constantly on Sara's "gentleness."

In lines first added to the "Monody on the Death of Chatterton" in 1796, the year after his marriage and when he still looked forward to going to America to establish Pantisocracy, he seems to reveal rather clearly the most he felt he could hope for from his marriage. He dares no longer muse on the sad theme of Chatterton's career,

> Lest kindred woes persuade a kindred doom:
> For oh! big gall-drops, shook from Folly's wing,
> Have blackened the fair promise of my spring;
> And the stern Fate transpierc'd with viewless dart
> The last pale Hope that shiver'd at my Heart!

The folly he speaks of was perhaps his debacle at Cambridge, involving the excursion into the cavalry, and his poor prospects as a result (if not, indeed, his involvement with Sara Fricker), the "last pale Hope" for something deeply significant to him, perhaps the possibility of marriage with Mary Evans, now married herself to someone else. But he continues:

> Hence, Gloomy thoughts! no more my soul shall dwell
> On joys that were! no more endure to weigh
> The shame and anguish of the evil day,
> Wisely forgetful! O'er the ocean swell
> Sublime of Hope I seek the cottag'd dell
> Where Virtue calm with careless step may stray;
> And, dancing to the moonlight roundelay,
> The wizard Passions weave a holy spell![23]

[22] *Poems*, p. 421.
[23] *Ibid.*, p. 130 (these eight lines formed the octet of the sonnet "Pantisocracy" [1794], in *Poems*, pp. 68-69).

This can only be characterized as pathetic bravado. Wisely, perhaps, but not very successfully forgetful he was to be. It is with a certain bravery as well as bravado that he resolves to accept calm virtue in place of having his visage read in his mind. He is depending also upon the passions, in the most ordinary sense of the word no doubt. But already he has passed into another world than that of the cottaged dell. His real and irrepressible ambitions have run away with his imagination, into the moonlit world (that most ubiquitous of all his symbols), and the passions are turned into wizards who will weave a *holy* spell. The ambiguities of this last line express with beautiful adequacy the ambiguity, not to say confusion, in Coleridge's mind at this point in his life. Elsewhere he speaks of the whole venture of Pantisocracy as something to "lull to sleep the Joys that were!"[24] But in fact, those joys had never been, had never at any rate been objectively realized.

A year or so after the Pantisocracy project had fallen by the wayside, Coleridge nevertheless found himself established in a "Cot o'ergrown / With white-flower'd Jasmin," still trying to convince himself (along with some high "hovering on untam'd wing") that all was well, and praising God,

> Who with his saving mercies healéd me,
> A sinful and most miserable man,
> Wilder'd and dark, and gave me to possess
> Peace, and this Cot, and thee heart-honour'd Maid![25]

In "Lines at Shurton Bars" (1795), having described a storm at the seashore in terms which bring "Dejection" to mind, he says,

> Even there—beneath that light-house tower—
> In the tumultuous evil hour
> *Ere Peace with Sara came,*

24 *Ibid.*, p. 63.
25 "The Eolian Harp" (1795), *ibid.*, p. 102.

> Time was, I should have thought it sweet
> To count the echoings of my feet,
> 　And watch the storm-vex'd flame.
> And there in black soul-jaundic'd fit
> A sad gloom-pamper'd Man to sit,
> 　And listen to the roar:
> When mountain surges bellowing deep
> With an uncouth monster-leap
> 　Plung'd foaming on the shore.[26]

No, his evil hours did not begin, as some have suggested, with the failure of his marriage, and the months of sympathy between him and Sara were at best an intermission. But it was easy for him at this moment, when he seemed to have reached his home, to speak with disdain of his "gloom-pamper'd" hours. The time was to come when he would think them sweet again. In "Dejection" he wishes for just such a storm, "Those sounds that oft have raised me, whilst they awed, / And sent my soul abroad," but it fails to send his soul abroad when it comes: the latter state is worse than the former.

A great deal may be said about Sara's responsibility for the failure of their marriage. Like Coleridge, she was in a way peculiarly, prophetically modern. In no sense an intellectual or an artist, she yet had a certain amount of contact with things intellectual and artistic. Not at all able, or willing, to forego her role as a woman in the way Dorothy Wordsworth had, to become one among the men, while retaining some of the great but not the essential advantages of womanhood, she had enough inkling of the things of the intellect to resent heartily the activities of a triumvirate like Coleridge, Wordsworth, and Dorothy. She was evidently lacking in sufficient passion to glory with confidence in her womanhood.[27] It was doubtless not that the Wordsworths

[26] *Ibid.*, p. 98 (italics mine).
[27] Miss Coburn called my attention to an entry in one of Coleridge's notebooks

alienated her husband's affections, (she must quickly have divined that Dorothy though perhaps in principle was not in fact a threat), but rather that the rapport among them shook her confidence in the ultimate value of her own role and sphere of interests. With that confidence shaken in this intangible but alarming manner, she may well have had misgivings as to her ability to "hold" a man like Coleridge. It would be very surprising if she did not sometimes say to herself—and even to Coleridge, "with the house and the baby to look after, *I* don't have the time or the energy to *observe nature*"—though with all the time and energy in the world she would surely have tired of doing so after five minutes. To buttress her position, there was the fact that no money came in. I have always been suspicious of Sara in the matter of that pan of hot milk she spilled on Coleridge's foot when Lamb was down from London and he and Coleridge and the Wordsworths were to go for a long walk in the country. If the suspicions are correct, Sara was "responsible" for at least one poem, "This Lime-Tree Bower My Prison," written while his friends were absent on their walk, if not, as some critics have

---

which strongly suggests that Sara was frigid. The note appears thus in Miss Coburn's edition of the *Notebooks* (Vol. I, entry 979, 21.131):

"Xd ⌈ Sara's . . . . . .
. . . interesting to trace it from its source in . . . .⌉
coldness perhaps & paralysis in all *tangible* ideas & sensations—all that forms *real Self*—hence ~~the Slave of her~~ she creates her own self in a field of Vision & Hearing, at a distance, by her own ears & eyes—& hence becomes the willing Slave of the Ears & Eyes of others.—Nothing affects her with pain ~~&~~ or pleasure as it is but only as other people will *say it is*—nay by an habitual absence of *reality* in her affections I have had an hundred instances that the being beloved, or the not being beloved, is a thing indifferent; but the *notion* of not being beloved—that wounds her pride deeply. ⌈ I have dressed perhaps washed ⌉ with her, & no one with us—all as cold & calm as a deep Frost—"

And, later in the same entry: "~~Sara~~ is uncommonly *cold* in her feelings of animal Love—G. H. is lustful—yet both are equally deficient in tangible Ideas & sensation—but G. H. I have not seen enough of to *understand* his character." G. H., Miss Coburn explains, is George Hutchinson, the brother of Mary Hutchinson Wordsworth and Sara Hutchinson.

suggested, for the other poems of the *annus mirabilis*. All Sara needed to be a typical twentieth-century suburban young matron was a college education.

But it will not do to be too hard on her. It may be that she was not even able to supply the possible, but Coleridge was quite evidently asking the impossible. Having alluded to the likelihood that Mrs. Coleridge was frigid (see note 27), there is no point in going on to suggest that Coleridge was himself impotent—there is evidence to the contrary. But although he presumably felt that sex had some place in life, and though he sometimes even speaks as if affection were really all he asked—"I could have been happy with a servant girl had she only in sincerity of heart responded to my affection"[28]—there are indications that he felt it had as little as possible to do with Love. A late work, "The Improvisatore" (1827), consists of a prose conversation between two girls and an older male friend who, in commenting on the song "Believe Me If All Those Endearing Young Charms" and some lines from Beaumont and Fletcher, expounds a doctrine of true love. The doctrine is familiar, and, though this statement of it is less extreme than some of Coleridge's utterances on the subject, one of the girls responds,

Well, Sir; you have said quite enough to make me despair of finding a 'John Anderson, my Jo, John', with whom to totter down the hill of life.[29]

At one point in the conversation, when the Friend is commencing his dissertation with the words,

Love, as distinguished from Friendship, on the one hand, and from the passion that too often usurps its name, on the other,

the brother of one of the girls suddenly appears and whispers to him, "But is not Love the union of both?" The Friend replies,

[28] Coburn, *Inquiring Spirit*, p. 304.
[29] *Poems*, p. 466.

"He never loved who thinks so," and the brother is unceremoniously sent out of the room, sent, to be exact, to help an otherwise unidentified Mrs. Hartman arrange a vase of flowers. That the Friend's view is Coleridge's own is confirmed by more explicit statements elsewhere. In a volume of Heinrich Steffens, opposite the words "bei dem Menschen, wo der Geschlechtstrieb sich zur Liebe verklärt," he notes:

I stand back from this! Love is the counteracting *contrary* of Lust and not the mere rarefaction of it. I hold in suspicion, rather I utterly denounce this Frenchery in all its fits, forms and fashions. As the sun to the dank vapors from the swamps so is Love to Lust, even in the fairest states of the latter.[30]

This is violent language, and the introduction of the word "Frenchery" gives further evidence that Coleridge was at the moment operating on the level of blind prejudice, glancing at something he could not bring himself to look straight in the eye. But he was also capable of making the same distinction more calmly. The following note was made on page 41 of *Die Metaphysik der Sitten in Zwei Teilen* (Königsberg, 1797):

This subject of Love, as not only contra-distinguished from Lust, but as disparate even from personal attachments of Habit and complex associations (sexual Desire of A determined exclusively to B by accidental freedom from other attachment and voluntary act of recalling of the form of B become at length an *in*voluntary *Habit* of the Memory: which is the description of the complex passion which passes for Love in a vast majority of instances)—in short, Love as different from Lust, from Friendship, from affection of Habit, and from the result of all three united in the same Object—of Love therefore, as an Element, this subject is one of the 5 or 6 Magna mysteria of human nature—[31]

[30] The passage is in *Karikaturen der Heiligsten,* II, 65. See Joseph Aynard, "Notes inédites de Coleridge," *Revue Germanique,* VII (1911), 301.

[31] Henri Nidecker, "Notes Marginales de S. T. Coleridge," *Revue de Littérature Comparée,* VII (1927), 338. Again the parallel with Poe, as Tate presents

No, it will not do to be too hard on Sara. The relationship between Coleridge and his wife might remind one of some lines of a modern American poet, John Crowe Ransom, which happen to describe Coleridge's situation at this point in his life with remarkable accuracy:

> So he stands muttering; and rushes
> Back to the tender thing in his charge
> With clamoring tongue and taste of ashes
> And a small passion to feign large.
>
> But let his cold lips be her omen
> She shall not kiss that harried one
> To peace, as men are served by women
> Who comfort them in darkness and in sun.[32]

And we recall his description of love as the "joy above the name of pleasure" in *The Triumph of Loyalty*. Earl Henry is referring to the woman he wooed "Hoping to heal a deeper wound"—precisely the status of Sara Fricker relative to Mary Evans in Coleridge's life. In the revised version ("The Night-Scene"), after Sandoval's sarcastic interruption comparing Earl Henry's conception of love to the Buddha's bliss, Earl Henry resumes:

> Ah! was that bliss
> Feared as an alien, and too vast for man?
> For suddenly, impatient of its silence,
> Did Oropeza, starting, grasp my forehead.
> I caught her arms; the veins were swelling on them.
> Through the dark bower she sent a hollow voice;—
> 'Oh! what if all betray me? What if thou?'[33]

---

him, is striking. Cf. *Forlorn Demon,* pp. 83-88. Tate observes that "If a writer ambiguously exalts the 'spirit' over the 'body', and the spirit must live wholly upon another spirit, some version of the vampire legend is likely to issue as the symbolic situation" (p. 88). Here we are inevitably reminded of *Christabel.*

[32] *Selected Poems* (New York: Alfred Knopf, 1945), p. 60.

[33] *Poems* p. 422.

And he rushes back to the bower to learn "Unwavering love, and singleness of heart."

There is a strikingly similar situation in another fragment, "The Ballad of the Dark Ladie" (1798). The lady appeals to the knight (also named Henry, incidentally) to shield and shelter her, since she has given him her all, and he replies, after promising her the fairest of nine castles,

> 'Wait only till the hand of eve
> Hath wholly closed yon western bars,
> And through the dark we two will steal
> Beneath the twinkling stars!'—

Her reaction is abrupt and terrified:

> 'The dark? the dark? No! not the dark?
> The twinkling stars? How, Henry? How?
> O God! 'twas in the eye of noon
> He pledged his sacred vow!'[34]

At least two other Coleridge ladies had difficulties with their lovers' becoming involuntarily estranged by some untoward experience. At the end of "The Three Graves" (1797-1809), Edward lies "with shut-up senses" while his wife and her friend watch the sun through the trees. They realize that he is having a nightmare (growing out of the previous events in the poem):

> Both groaned at once, for both knew well
> What thoughts were in his mind;
> When he waked up, and stared like one
> That hath been just struck blind.

> He sat upright; and ere the dream
> Had had time to depart,
> 'O God, forgive me'! (he exclaimed)
> 'I have torn out her heart.'

[34] *Ibid.*, p. 294.

> Then Ellen shrieked, and forthwith burst
> Into ungentle laughter;
> And Mary shivered, where she sat,
> And never she smiled after.[35]

The knight in the fragmentary tale recounted in "Love" (1799), crazed in this instance by his lady's scorn, suffers a recurrent hallucination in the form of "an angel beautiful and bright" whom he knows to be in fact a Fiend. The lady nurses him back to sanity, but only at the moment of his death.

Is it too much to see all of these as more or less remote versions of the "demon lover" whom the woman is wailing for in "Kubla Khan," haunting the deep romantic chasm which slanted down the green hill near the pleasure-dome, a "savage place," "holy and enchanted"? The Dark Ladie, for one, was also waiting by a brook that "falls scattered down the rock," near a "castled mountain." And Earl Henry thus describes the scene in *The Triumph of Loyalty*:

> Within this wood there winds a secret passage,
> Beneath the walls, which opens out at length
> Into the gloomiest covert of the Garden.—[36]

It is the garden of a castle, hard by a stream, and the atmosphere, somewhat like that in "Kubla Khan," is, to borrow a word from Miss Schneider's analysis of that poem, a kind of oscillation between gloom and brightness, fear and pleasure.

The theme is thus a recurrent one in Coleridge's poetry, and some significance may be seen in the fact that in every instance it occurs in a "fragment." Perhaps Coleridge was never able to work it out in poetry because he never worked it out in his own experience—it always remained one of the *Magna mysteria*. As we have seen, he really made no lasting attempt to realize what

[35] *Ibid.*, p. 284.
[36] *Ibid.*, p. 568.

he sought from love with Sara Fricker. While he was still trying to be enthusiastic about the union, he saw it as a flight into calm domestic peace. If Sara caught a glimpse of what he was after, and she must have, he doubtless seemed to her something of a monster.

But he was to be no more successful in achieving his ultimate ambition with a much more likely subject, the great love of his life, Sara Hutchinson. However important on one level Coleridge's failure to achieve fulfillment in love may have been in frustrating his poetic activity, what seems more important, more revealing, is the degree to which his failure in love can be traced to a common root with the frustration of his poetic activity. The suggestion is that he was looking for the same thing from love and from poetic experience, namely, a religious, a mystical experience of the absolute, and that he failed to find it in both for the same reason, because it is not there to find.

Ordinary disappointment in love does not necessarily produce poetic inhibition—the contrary is frequently the case, as with Dante. But when Coleridge cites his own frustration in love as a cause of his poetic inhibition, he is by no means just making an irrelevant excuse. The connection between the two was very real and very profound—the same overweening ambition underlay them both. In the same poem in which he cries out, "Why was I made for Love and Love denied to me?" the following stanza occurs:

> Imagination; honourable aims;
> Free commune with the choir that cannot die;
> Science and song; delight in little things,
> The buoyant child surviving in the man;
> Fields, forests, ancient mountains, ocean, sky,
> With all their voices—O dare I accuse
> My earthly lot as guilty of my spleen,
> Or call my destiny niggard! O no! no!

It is her largeness and her overflow,
Which being incomplete, disquieteth me so![37]

One is reminded of Hopkins—Coleridge seems to be saying

Thou art indeed just, Lord, if I contend
With thee; but, sir, so what I plead is just.

And the whole of this sonnet of Hopkins is strikingly reminiscent of Coleridge's sonnet "Work Without Hope." A fulfillment in love, Coleridge felt, would have made up the full measure, and would have enabled him to realize the potentialities of his other gifts:

Crown of his cup, and garnish of his dish!
The boon, prefigured in his earliest wish,
The fair fulfillment of his poesy,
When his young heart first yearn'd for sympathy![38]

It would surely have made him a happier man, and possibly therefore a more successful one—he would, in short, have been a quite different man, and speculations on the subject are idle. In fact, the largeness and the overflow cracked the vessel of love, and the vessel of poetry. In his prose recollection of the lost opening stanzas of "The Blossoming of the Solitary Date-Tree" (1805), he puts it in this way:

The finer the sense for the beautiful and the lovely, and the fairer and lovelier the object presented to the sense; the more exquisite the individual's capacity for joy, and the more ample his means and opportunities of enjoyment, the more heavily will he feel the ache of solitariness, the more unsubstantial becomes the feast spread around him. What matters it, whether in fact the viands and the ministering graces are shadowy or real, to him who has not hand to grasp nor arms to embrace them? [39]

---

[37] *Poems,* p. 396 ("The Blossoming of the Solitary Date-Tree," lines 48-57).
[38] *Ibid.,* p. 467 ("The Improvisatore," lines 5-8).
[39] *Ibid.,* p. 396.

But this recollection took place when he was preparing the 1828 edition of his poems, and reflects the attitude of his more advanced years. In 1798, when he was giving to poetry all he had (and asking of it more than it had to give him), although he already knew that his marriage would not bring fulfillment, he was still capable of an ecstasy of poetic ambition, still confident of the Ministrations of Nature; and encouraged by warm, understanding friendship, he sought his fulfillment with Wordsworth, in mystical communion with nature, in the poetic experience. But by 1802, when "Dejection" was written, he knew that here also were no "wings of healing" for him.

Yet although failure in love cannot be considered the *cause* of the fading of his poetic gifts since his first great disappointment in love antedated his period of greatest poetic activity by several years, and the bloom was almost certainly off his marriage after two years (by 1797), there is still an important relation between the two, which must be explored further in the light of developments that followed his meeting with Sara Hutchinson. The course of this relationship has been traced in very complete detail by Professor George Whalley in *Coleridge and Sara Hutchinson and the Asra Poems*.[40] They met in 1799 at the home of her brother at Sockburn-on-Tees, where Coleridge had gone to meet the Wordsworths. Sara was the sister of Mary Hutchinson, who became the wife of Wordsworth in 1802. (In order to avoid the possible confusion resulting from the identity of given names between Sara Hutchinson and Coleridge's wife, Sara Fricker, the former will be referred to under the name of *Asra*, Coleridge's anagram for her name.) The evidence is that Coleridge fell in love with her very nearly at first sight, in any case at first meeting, and that she in some fashion returned his love. The relationship continued through different phases for some

[40] London: Routledge & Kegan Paul Ltd., 1955.

ten years before they finally ceased to communicate with each other; the probability seems to be that their love was never consummated. Certainly the relationship was a very profound one on Coleridge's part, and doubtless on hers as well.[41] If Coleridge's hope for crucial fulfillment in love seems to have outlasted poetic ambition of the same order, it is perhaps because love's success or failure seemed in spite of everything to depend so much more immediately on an outside object, and a finally unpredictable one. In fact, in terms of results produced, love failed long before poetry—it never succeeded, never produced results. It was the capacity to hope for them that seems to have endured longer.

It is only in his later poems, like "Constancy to an Ideal Object" (1826?), that he makes observations about love that are comparable to what "Dejection" says about poetry. But there is a fragment of just three lines composed in 1803 which seems extraordinarily acute in its suggested analysis of his situation in the early days of his acquaintance with Asra:

> My irritable fears all sprang from Love—
> Suffer that fear to strengthen it—Give way
> And let it work—'twill fix the Love it springs from.[42]

The interpretation I am suggesting of these rather curious lines is this: the irritable fears in question, which sprang from love, were fears of giving himself to something he unwillingly foreknew could not offer what he sought from it. A merely human love could not satisfy his supernal longings, and he shied away from it while longing for it. One would never guess from other passages we have cited, especially from his expressions of love for Asra, that there was any problem about commitment—he seems

---

[41] Very little is known first-hand concerning Asra's reactions. Nearly all the correspondence between them has been lost, so that we have only Coleridge's side, revealed in poems, letters to other people, and notebooks.

[42] Reprinted by Whalley, *Coleridge and Asra*, p. 169, from J. D. Campbell's edition of the *Poetic Works*, (London and New York: Macmillan, 1909), p. 460.

utterly committed. But in those passages, I think, he is talking incautiously about what he *wants,* with hardly more than incidental reference to the person in question, to the actual experience of simple human love he might conceivably have achieved with her. In this fragment, however, his ideal of love and the actual human possibility do confront each other.[43] When he says "My irritable fears all sprang from Love," I believe "Love" refers to the complex, to the impossible mystical aspiration *and* the human possibility—it is out of the conflict between the aspiration and the possibility that the fears spring. When he admonishes himself, "Suffer that fear to strengthen it," "it" is the human love. If he *faces* the fear that human love will not live up to his aspiration, that fear will be exorcised, and he will be able to face the impossibility of attaining the absolute and so relax into the possible, accept an actually attainable human relation. "'Twill *fix* the Love it springs from" he says—"fix" it perhaps on a particular human person. The fear, faced through to the very end, will bring love down to earth and make something viable of it. And recall the fragment quoted earlier:

> O Joy! with thy own joy at strife,
> > That yearning for the Realm above
> Wouldst die into intenser Life,
> > And union absolute of Love![44]

---

[43] As they do in still another fragment where he speaks of
> O th' Oppressive, irksome weight
> Felt in an uncertain state:
> Comfort, peace, and rest adieu
> Should I prove at last untrue!

> Self-confiding wretch, I thought
> I could love thee as I ought,
> Win thee and deserve to feel
> All the love thou canst reveal,
> And still I chuse thee, follow still.

(*Poems,* p. 497)

[44] *Poems,* p. 501. See in this book p. 32.

Coleridge's more or less conventional (and more or less justified) complaints about Asra's indifference or unresponsiveness pale in significance beside these fragments, which offer a glimpse into the elements in Coleridge's own personality that were at the root of his failure in love.

Doubtless it is these same "fears" that recur in the self-recriminating passage in "To William Wordsworth" (1807). Hearing Wordsworth read his *Prelude* had "roused a throng of pains":

> Keen pangs of Love, awakening as a babe
> Turbulent, with an outcry in the heart;
> And fears self-willed, that shunned the eye of Hope;
> And Hope that scarce would know itself from Fear.[45]

In commenting on the passage in connection with Asra, Whalley remarks that "What these 'fears self-willed, that shunned the eye of Hope' may have been we cannot guess; for Asra was at this time his last image of hope."[46] But perhaps we *can* guess that they were fears aroused precisely because of the extravagance of the hope—premonitory, self-protective fears. Miss Coburn has published a manuscript note in which Coleridge discusses at some length the role of fear in his life, saying that "it is a most instructive part of my Life the fact, that I have been always preyed on by some Dread." He lists various fears, beginning with his childhood, and what he says about the element of fear in his relationship with Mary Evans *is* "most instructive." He speaks of

a state of struggling with madness from an incapability of hoping that I should be able to marry Mary Evans (and this strange passion of fervent tho' wholly imaginative and imaginary Love uncombinable by my utmost efforts with any regular Hope—possibly from deficiency of bodily feeling, of tactual ideas connected with the image) had all the

---

[45] *Poems*, p. 407.
[46] *Coleridge and Asra*, p. 133.

effects of direct Fear, and I have lain for hours together awake at night, groaning and praying.[47]

We are immediately reminded of the poem "Phantom," written with Asra in mind, and quoted by Coleridge "to illustrate the idea that the love-sense can be abstracted from the accidents of form and person," and thence of his definition of beauty, drawn from Pythagoras and the mystics—and its results, expounded in "Dejection."

A poem dating from 1802 describes a brief interlude when he was able, again with a kind of bravado, to escape the fears, by resolutely turning his back on love. It was probably written while he was taking an extended walking tour alone through the Lake District, and is entitled "The Picture, or the Lover's Resolution."

> Through weeds and thorns, and matted underwood
> I *force* my way; now climb, and now descend
> O'er rocks, or bare or mossy, with *wild foot*
> *Crushing* the purple whorts; while oft *unseen,*
> The scared snake rustles. Onward still I toil,
> *I know not, ask not whither!* A *new* joy,
> Lovely as light, sudden as summer gust,
> And gladsome as the first-born of the spring,
> Beckons me on, or follows from behind,
> *Playmate,* or guide![48]

In an earlier version, the "wild foot" was a "blind foot." The joy he feels is a "new" joy, achieved by virtue of a kind of blindness, indifference, unaskingness, significantly different, one may suppose, from the lost Joy of "Dejection," "Which wedding Nature to us gives in dower." "The master-passion quelled," he says, "I feel that I am free," and he dismisses

[47] *Inquiring Spirit,* p. 54.
[48] *Poems,* p. 369 (italics mine).

> the love-lorn man, who, sick in soul,
> And of this busy human heart aweary,
> Worships the spirit of unconscious life
> In tree or wild-flower. —Gentle lunatic!
>
> If so he might not wholly cease to be,
> He would far rather not be that he is;
> He would be something that he knows not of,
> In winds or waters, or among the rocks![49]

The mystical communion with nature, here seen as something negative, an escape from the pains of disappointed love, is dismissed as unnecessary.

> This is my hour of triumph! I can now
> With my own fancies play the merry fool,
> And laugh away worse folly, being free.[50]

He would seem here to be trying to capture the mood of unreflective youthful spontaneity which Wordsworth describes in detail in "Tintern Abbey" as one of his outgrown stages:

> And so I dare to hope,
> Though changed, no doubt, from what I was when first
> I came among these hills; when like a roe
> I bounded o'er the mountains, by the sides
> Of the deep rivers, and the lonely streams,

---

[49] *Ibid.*, pp. 369-70. Cf. fragment 19, *ibid.*, p. 498, and T. S. Eliot's lines,

> I should have been a pair of ragged claws
> Scuttling across the floors of silent seas.

As a matter of fact, it may not be too much to see in Coleridge's lapse of sensibility a forecast of the predicament of J. Alfred Prufrock. One thinks especially of Prufrock's wondering whether it would have been worthwhile

> To have squeezed the universe into a ball
> To roll it toward some overwhelming question,
> To say: 'I am Lazarus come from the dead,
> Come back to tell you all, I shall tell you all'—
> If one, settling a pillow by her head,
> Should say: 'That is not what I meant at all.
>   That is not it at all.'

[50] *Poems*, p. 370.

> Wherever nature led: more like a man
> Flying from something that he dreads than one
> Who sought the thing he loved. For nature then
> (The coarser pleasures of my boyish days,
> And their glad animal movements all gone by)
> To me was all in all. —I cannot paint
> What then I was. The sounding cataract
> Haunted me like a passion: the tall rock,
> The mountain, and the deep and gloomy wood,
> Their colors and their forms, were then to me
> An appetite; a feeling and a love,
> That had no need of a remoter charm,
> By thought supplied, nor any interest
> Unborrowed from the eye.[51]

Even Coleridge's flight from the human element felt in nature, being "of this busy human heart aweary," into a "silent shade"

> As safe and sacred from the step of man
> As an invisible world—unheard, unseen,

finds its counterpart in Wordsworth's description of his own out-grown youth, before he had learned to hear the "still, sad music of humanity" in looking upon nature. There follows immediately in Wordsworth's poem the famous passage about "something far more deeply interfused." The mood Coleridge describes in "The Picture" is a flight from all of this, a futilely attempted regression to a former state of innocence—if indeed Coleridge had ever been so innocent as that. And we may also be reminded of his earlier attempt, in "Shurton Bars," to convince himself that he had escaped his compulsion to the absolute in the arms of Sara Fricker.

A section of the same poem, interesting from another point of view, describes an imaginary lover, who might watch his be-loved's image mirrored in the stream beside which the poet finds himself.

[51] Lines 65-83.

Who erewhile
Had from her countenance turned, or looked by stealth
(For Fear is true-love's cruel nurse), he now
With steadfast gaze and unoffending eye,
Worships the watery idol, dreaming hopes
Delicious to the soul, but fleeting, vain,
E'en as that phantom-world on which he gazed.[52]

And we remember the later poem "Phantom." Here, quite appropriately, it is the real maiden, displeased or frightened at being worshiped as an idol, who destroys the phantom one—by throwing some flowers onto the surface of the pool.

Then all the charm
Is broken—all that phantom world so fair
Vanishes, and a thousand circlets spread,
And each mis-shape the other.[53]

When the surface calms, the maiden has disappeared, "Homeward she steals through many a woodland maze / Which he shall seek in vain." Somewhat like Coleridge, instead of going after the real maiden, the imaginary lover wastes his "manly prime"

In mad love-yearning by the vacant brook,
Till sickly thoughts bewitch thine eyes, and thou
Behold'st her shadow still abiding there,
The Naiad of the mirror![54]

This is certainly a rather obvious description of what, in the terms of Fairchild, James, and others,[55] may be called a "flight from reality." It is not "normal" behavior, and probably falls within some quite elementary psychiatric category. No doubt there were some very ordinary, mundane factors in Coleridge's early life, perhaps also some innate flaws in his character, which

[52] *Poems,* p. 371, lines 79-85.
[53] *Ibid.,* p. 371, lines 91-94.
[54] *Ibid.,* lines 108-11.
[55] See in this book pp. 8 ff.

contributed to his hesitancy to approach a real maiden with confidence as the embodiment of his ideal, as a fulfillment of his deepest personal needs. But if this is so, it by no means nullifies the significance of the aberration on another level. If it represents a flight *from* reality, it may also represent a flight *to* a higher reality, or to the dream of a higher reality. To go to the ultimate extreme for an analogy, the lives of the saints are no less authentically saintly because, since saints are also poor human beings, they approach purity and union with God through a welter of very human causes.

Coleridge quotes lines 91-100 of "The Picture"[56] in the prefatory note to "Kubla Khan" as a poetic description of what supposedly happened when the person from Porlock interrupted the transcription of the dreamed poem. There is an interesting relation between the maidens in the two poems. The Abyssinian maid, once seen in a vision, is another Naiad of the mirror, another Phantom.[57] Could he revive within him her symphony and song, he would be able to build the pleasure-dome—but, as a result,

> all should cry, Beware! Beware!
> His flashing eyes, his floating hair!
> Weave a circle round him thrice
> And close your eyes with holy dread,
> For he on honey-dew hath fed,
> And drunk the milk of Paradise.[58]

"All"—including any real maiden in whom he tried to see the phantom.

Whalley quotes a notebook entry written late in 1808, which is obviously a sketch for a poem that was never written:

56 Quoted on p. 50 in this book.
57 See in this book pp. 30-31.
58 *Poems*, p. 298.

'My Angel'!—Nay, I am no Angel / have no wings, no glory / but flesh & Blood—The Lover's Answer, from playful to tender & from tender to grave / Sara.[59]

And he cites other instances in which Coleridge refers to Asra as an angel. It must be remembered that Coleridge, being theologically sophisticated, uses the word "angel" not as a trite term of endearment but in full consciousness of its technical definition—this is evident in a note first published in *Anima Poetae:* "For compassion a human Heart suffices; but for full adequate sympathy with Joy an angel's—"[60] Among the notes published by T. M. Raysor is one in which Coleridge says,

I have *loved* so as I should feel no shame to describe to an Angel, and as my experience makes me suspect—to an Angel alone would be intelligible.[61]

But it took Coleridge a long time to act on that experience, and, as we shall see, the action finally produced took the form of resignation rather than readjustment. It would seem that Coleridge never quite came to the explicit realization of what he was doing that is expressed by Gérard de Nerval when he says:

I understand, I said to myself, I have preferred the creature to the creator; I have deified my love and worshiped according to pagan rites her whose last breath was offered up to Christ. But if that religion is true God can still forgive me.[62]

The mood recorded in "The Picture" was in any case very short-lived, as was his "Farewell to Love" in 1806—a very short

---

[59] *Coleridge and Asra*, p. 137 (from N 13, f. 21).

[60] *Ibid.*, p. 282 (from N 22, f. 62v). Tate entitles one of his essays on Poe "The Angelic Imagination: Poe as God" (*Forlorn Demon*, pp. 56-78), and therein refers to Coleridge's " 'esemplastic power' of the Primary Imagination, a Teutonic angel inhabiting a Cartesian machine named Samuel Taylor Coleridge."

[61] *Coleridge and Asra*, p. 323.

[62] *Oeuvres Choisies* (Lausanne: Henri Kaeser, 1948), p. 304 (translation mine).

time later he was again "Plucking the poisons of self-harm." [63]
Whalley identifies "Psyche" (1808) as an "Asra poem":

> The butterfly the ancient Grecians made
> The soul's fair emblem, and its only name—
> But of the soul, escaped the slavish trade
> Of mortal life!—For in this earthly frame
> Ours is the reptile's lot, much toil, much blame,
> Manifold motions making little speed,
> And to deform and kill the things whereon we feed. [64]

He remarks,

It would seem that in his mind the ambivalent symbol of the butterfly
could easily associate itself with the poised ambivalence of that love in
which 'the truly beloved is the *symbol* of God.' In *Psyche* he expresses
with appalling directness the grim discovery that, if perfect love is
perfectly creative, imperfect love can be devastatingly destructive. This
lesson, one would suppose, he had already learned as a young man;
in the Coleorton days he was relearning it to his irremediable
sorrow. [65]

If, as seems very likely, Whalley is correct that Coleridge was
thinking of love in writing this poem, I believe the contrast is
being drawn not between perfect and imperfect love, in the
sense of fulfilled and unfulfilled love, but rather between love as
it would exist for a disembodied spirit and love as it exists "in
this earthly frame." The implication is that *any* love within this
earthly frame deforms and kills the things whereon it feeds—
and so it does, no doubt, if it is trying to be the kind of love appropriate only to a disembodied soul! And this is a lesson which,
as we have seen, Coleridge by no means learned as a young man.

The idea that one has always known the loved one is not un-

[63] *Poems*, p. 407, "To William Wordsworth" (1807).
[64] *Ibid.*, p. 412.
[65] *Coleridge and Asra*, p. 133.

common among lovers, and Coleridge alludes to it many times,
but most explicitly in "Recollections of Love" (1807—), stanza iv:

> As when a mother doth explore
> The rose-mark on her long-lost child,
> I met, I loved you, maiden mild!
> As whom I long had loved before—
> So deeply had I been beguiled.[66]

At some later date (Whalley suggests the summer of 1810[67]), he
added two more stanzas to the poem, the first of which begins:

> You stood before me like a thought,
> A dream remembered in a dream.

Again we are reminded of the Abyssinian maid, the vision remembered in the dream of "Kubla Khan." There is a whole
series of women wailing for their demon-lovers in Coleridge's
poems; and to correspond to them there is a series of demon-
lovers wailing for the embodiment of their demon-love in a flesh-
and-blood woman. Coleridge is touching here, in his poetry and
in the personal experience behind it, upon one of the most ancient
of mythological themes—love between a human being and a god.
In the myths the human consequences were most often disas-
trous. Coleridge would surely have understood what Rimbaud
meant when he said:

I am slave to the infernal Bridegroom, the one who was the undoing
of the foolish virgins. He is really that very demon. He is not a ghost,
he is not a phanton.[68]

Both of them can truly say that for them "love has to be rein-
vented."

66 *Poems,* pp. 409-10.
67 *Coleridge and Asra,* p. 137n.
68 *A Season in Hell,* trans. by Louise Varese (Norfolk: New Directions, 1952),
p. 37. Unless otherwise indicated, all quotations from the work are taken from
this translation.

At the time of the definitive break with Asra, around 1810, Coleridge's reaction was one of desperation, to the point of thinking of suicide:

> I have experienced
> The worst the world can wreak on me—the worst
> That can make Life indifferent, yet disturb
> With whisper'd discontent the dying prayer—
> I have beheld the whole of all, wherein
> *My* heart had any interest in this life
> To be disrent and torn from off my Hopes
> That nothing now is left. Why then live on?
> That hostage that the world had in its keeping
> Given by me as a pledge that I would live—
> That hope of Her, say rather that pure Faith
> In her fix'd Love, which held me to keep truce
> With the tyranny of Life—is gone, ah! whither?
> What boots it to reply? 'tis gone! and now
> Well may I break this Pact, this league of Blood
> That ties me to myself—and break I shall.[69]

Three years before he had already written (and published, as Whalley points out, "to the intense disapproval of his wife and Southey"[70]), that "Hope long is dead to me,"[71] but it had not yet been quite true. Now there was no doubt of it. The idea of suicide was still in his mind in 1811, when he composed "The Suicide's Argument," which in a notebook he prefaced with the lines:

> Complained of, complaining, there shov'd and here shoving,
> Every one blaming me, ne'er a one loving.[72]

But "nature's answer" to the project of suicide was, "Then die— if die you dare!", and Coleridge did not dare. And thenceforward

[69] *Poems*, pp. 501-2, fragment 35.
[70] *Coleridge and Asra*, p. 131.
[71] *Poems*, p. 412, "To Two Sisters."
[72] *Ibid.*, p. 419*n*.

a new atmosphere informs the relatively few poems he wrote, an atmosphere of remoteness, nostalgia, calm melancholy, sometimes so deep that he can even be a little playful with it. The attitude that he had tried in vain to adopt in 1802 when he wrote "The Picture" is finally achieved. It may be permitted to identify the quality of these later poems as Yeatsian—one might point to a whole series of these later poems, culminating in "The Garden of Boccaccio," Coleridge's version of "Sailing to Byzantium." There is even, in a little song from *Zapolya,* a bird of gold and amethyst, and the song itself strikes something like the same note:

> A sunny shaft did I behold,
>   From sky to earth it slanted:
> And poised therein a bird so bold—
>   Sweet bird, thou wert enchanted!
>
> He sank, he rose, he twinkled, he trolled
>   Within the shaft of sunny mist;
> His eyes of fire, his beak of gold,
>   All else of amethyst!
>
> And thus he sang: 'Adieu! Adieu!
> Love's dreams prove seldom true.
> The blossoms they make no delay:
> The sparkling dew-drops will not stay.
>   Sweet month of May,
>   We must away;
>   Far, far away!
>   Today! today!'[73]

Whalley points out a specific Shakespearean echo in a much earlier poem about a bird, "The Nightingale," which, as he says, is a merry poem.[74] It deserves contrast with this little song, in

[73] *Ibid.,* pp. 426-27.
[74] *Coleridge and Asra,* pp. 114-15.

which Coleridge approaches the rare quality of Shakespeare's songs, the melancholy words sung to a lightsome tune.

The first old man's poem is "Youth and Age" (1823-32), in which Yeats might have found some of his favorite themes. Is not

> This breathing house not built with hands,
> This body that does me grievous wrong,[75]

surely the same as

> this caricature,
> Decrepit age that has been tied to me
> As to a dog's tail?[76]

Yeats goes on to say,

> Never had I more
> Excited, passionate, fantastical
> Imagination, nor an ear and eye
> That more expected the impossible—
> No, not in boyhood when with rod and fly
> Or the humbler worm, I climbed Ben Bulben's back.[77]

Similarly, Coleridge finds it in one way difficult to believe in the reality of age:

> O Youth! for years so many and sweet,
> 'Tis known that Thou and I were one,
> I'll think it but a fond conceit—
> It cannot be that thou art gone!
> Thy vesper-bell hath not yet toll'd:—
> And thou wert aye a masker bold!
> What strange disguise hast now put on,
> To make believe, that thou art gone?
> I see these locks in silvery slips,
> This drooping gait, this altered size:

---

[75] *Poems*, p. 429.
[76] "The Tower," *Collected Poems* (New York: Macmillan, 1942), p. 224.
[77] *Ibid.*

But springtide blossoms on my lips,
And tears take sunshine from thine eyes!
Life is but thought: so think I will
That Youth and I are house-mates still.[78]

In concluding lines, published a few years later, he has not yet fully arrived at the point where he can say with Yeats:

I have prepared my peace
With learned Italian things
And the proud stones of Greece,
Poet's imaginings
And memories of love,
Memories of the words of women,
And those things whereof
Man makes a superhuman
Mirror-resembling dream.[79]

But this is what he does say:

Where no hope is, life's a warning
That only serves to make us grieve,
              When we are old:

That only serves to make us grieve
With oft and tedious taking-leave,
Like some poor nigh-related guest,
That may not rudely be dismissed;
Yet hath outstay'd his welcome while,
And tells the jest without a smile.[80]

This is like a version of Yeats' epigram "Youth and Age":

Much did I rage when young,
Being by the world oppressed,
But now with flattering tongue
It speeds the parting guest.[81]

[78] *Poems*, p. 440.
[79] *Collected Poems*, pp. 229-30.
[80] *Poems*, pp. 440-41.
[81] *Collected Poems*, p. 244.

Finally, in "Constancy to an Ideal Object" (1826?), we find full resignation, and a kind of recognition, already reflected in the title, that he had all along been asking of flesh and blood the impossible:

> Since all that beat about in Nature's range,
> Or veer or vanish; why should'st thou remain
> The only constant in a world of change,
> O yearning Thought! that liv'st but in the brain?

The answer is in reality contained in the question.

> Yet still thou haunt'st me; and though well I see,
> She is not thou, and only thou art she,
> Still, still as though some dear embodied Good,
> Some living Love before my eyes there stood
> With answering look a ready ear to lend,
> I mourn to thee. . . .
>
> And art thou nothing? Such thou art, as when
> The woodman winding westward up the glen
> At wintry dawn, where o'er the sheep-track's maze
> The viewless snow-mist weaves a glist'ning haze,
> Sees full before him, gliding without tread,
> An image with a glory round its head;
> The enamoured rustic worships its fair hues,
> Nor knows he makes the shadow, he pursues![82]

Here he is finally saying in relation to love something comparable to what he had first said more than twenty years before in relation to poetry:

> O Sara! we receive but what we give,
> And in *our* life alone does Nature live.

A year or so later, in 1827, he was to write "The Improvisatore," in which not only resignation but a kind of peace is recorded.

[82] *Poems,* pp. 455-56.

When the Friend has finished his disquisition on true love, one of the girls responds with the question:

Eliz. Surely, he, who has described it so well, must have possessed it?

Fri. If he were worthy to have possessed it, and had believingly anticipated and not found it, how bitter the disappointment!

He pauses for a few minutes, and then couches his full reply in a 67-line poem "ex improviso" which begins:

> Yes, yes! that boon, life's richest treat
> He had, or fancied that he had;
> Say, 'twas but in his own conceit—
>   The fancy made him glad!
> Crown of his cup, and garnish of his dish!
> The boon, prefigured in his earliest wish,
> The fair fulfillment of his poesy,
> When his young heart first yearn'd for sympathy!
> But e'en the meteor offspring of the brain
>   Unnourished wane;
> Faith asks her daily bread,
> And Fancy must be fed!

He describes its slow death,

> That boon, which but to have possess'd
> In a *belief,* gave life a zest— . . . .
> Poor shadow cast from an unsteady wish,
> Itself a substance by no other right
> But that it intercepted Reason's light;
> It dimm'd his eye, it darken'd on his brow,
> A peevish mood, a tedious time, I trow!
>   Thank Heaven! 'tis not so now.[83]

And in closing Coleridge sings his final paean to love:

> O bliss of blissful hours!
> The boon of Heaven's decreeing,

[83] *Ibid.,* pp. 467-68.

> While yet in Eden's bowers
> Dwelt the first husband and his sinless mate!
> The one sweet plant, which, piteous Heaven agreeing,
> They bore with them thro' Eden's closing gate!
> Of life's gay summer tide the sovran Rose!
> Late autumn's Amaranth, that more fragrant blows
> When Passion's flowers all fall and fade;
> If this were ever his, in outward being,
> Or but his own true love's projected shade,
> Now that at length by certain proof he knows,
> That whether real or magic show,
> Whate'er it *was,* it *is* no longer so;
> Though heart be lonesome, Hope laid low,
> Yet, Lady! deem him not unblest:
> The certainty that struck Hope dead,
> Hath left Contentment in her stead:
>   And that is next to Best![84]

For Coleridge, at any rate, the mistake was to have supposed what he sought had been allowed "thro' Eden's closing gate!"

Note. In discussing the significance of love in Coleridge's life, I have deliberately ignored one whole level of possible interpretation—the psychoanalytic level. But something must be said on the subject, since there are several reasons for having ignored it, among which is not numbered the assumption that it is irrelevant, that psycho-analysis has nothing significant to contribute to the understanding of Coleridge's personality. Perhaps the primary reason for having ignored it is that I am capable neither of making the analysis myself, nor of assessing with confidence the worth of attempts that have been made.

Coleridge's life obviously offers a rich field for such analyses, and a number have been undertaken, which, to the layman's eye, vary greatly in degree of probability and apparent relevance. Among the less probable and relevant analyses, I should say, is an article by H. S. and D. T. Bliss on "Coleridge's 'Kubla Khan',"[85] in which the vari-

---

[84] *Ibid.,* p. 468.
[85] *American Imago,* VI, No. 4 (1949), 261-73.

ous images in that poem are translated into what appear to be some-what stereotyped equivalents (e.g. "cedarn cover" = pubic hair); and the conclusion is reached that Coleridge gave up poetry because he was shocked by its sexual nature. I suspect that many psycho-analysts would agree that post-mortem analyses are of questionable validity at best, but some serious effort should at least be made to determine the special significance of a given image for the individ-ual under analysis.

A more interesting and rewarding study is that of David Beres, "A Dream, a Vision, and a Poem: a Psychoanalytic Study of the Origins of the *Rime of the Ancient Mariner,*"[86] although Beres some-what surprisingly accepts without criticism Lowes' simple associa-tionist conception of the poetic process. He diagnoses Coleridge as an "oral character," and finds the most significant cause of his neurosis in the fact that he was unloved by his mother. As a result, he turned to reading, phantasy, and food, and sought in love the protection of a mother:

"Coleridge did not permit his hostile feeling to his mother to come to the surface of his conscious mind. He repressed in his unconscious mind his conflicted ambivalent emotions about her, his crying need, his bitter frustration, and his guilt at the hate this must have engen-dered. The repressed emotions and conflicts came to consciousness only in distorted and unrecognizable forms. They appeared in his rela-tionships to other persons—his demands on people, his unrealistic loves and his distressing behavior toward his wife. They also appeared in the symbolism and imagery of his poetry."[87]

From what is known of Coleridge's life, even from the few facts cited in this chapter, it would seem likely that this diagnosis has considerable validity. It proceeds, at any rate, from known or plausibly surmised facts, instead of applying *a priori* psychoanalytical cate-gories to isolated images from the poems; and it avoids the over-simplification which would reduce the whole thing to saying some-thing like, *The Ancient Mariner* is what it is because Coleridge hated his mother.

The fact is that a number of neurotic symptoms can plausibly be

[86] *International Journal of Psycho-Analysis,* XXXII, No. 2 (1951), 97-116.
[87] *Ibid.,* p. 104.

attributed to Coleridge (he describes some of them himself with surprising clinical accuracy)—an inverted mother complex, latent homosexuality, hypochrondria, depression; and the recognition of them in these clinical terms might conceivably be of great assistance in understanding the man and his works, *if* we understand the terms themselves well enough, *if* we do not fall into the reduction fallacy, and *if* we do not suppose diagnosis in clinical terms to imply something like condemnation, or like dismissal as "abnormal."

But the important question for us here is, what is the relation between such a diagnosis, even supposing it to be quite accurate, and the "diagnosis," the line of analysis, here pursued, which tends to interpret the facts in "religious" terms? It is not a question that will, or can, be settled here, because that would require a final decision as to the relation between the psychoanalytic and religious frames of reference. I suggest simply that the least plausible decision would be that either *superseded* the other. Just as I think it would occur to no responsible theologian to suppose he could fix certain limits within which are to be found the instrumentalities of contact between man and God, so I should think it would occur to no responsible psycho-analyst to suppose that his therapeutically oriented interpretation of the facts of a man's life exhausts the significance of those facts. If either does hold such a view, it derives from something other than his professional competence.

III

SYMBOLS OF
IMAGINATION

Of all Coleridge's poems, leaving out the big three, none is more frequently referred to and discussed than "Dejection: An Ode" (1802).[1] But although one critic calls it the best of his poems,[2] it owes most of its critical popularity to its status as a document in Coleridge's spiritual biography.

Coleridge prefaced "Dejection" with this stanza from "The Ballad of Sir Patrick Spence":

> Late, late yestreen I saw the new Moon
> With the old Moon in her arms;
> And I fear, I fear, my Master dear!
> We shall have a deadly storm.

He thereby put into our hands an important key to the interpretation of his poem, since his use of these symbols, the moon and the storm, dates from his earliest verse. In tracing their use, both separately and together, up to the time of "Dejection," it ought to be possible to establish with some certainty the force they may be expected to have in this poem, and at the same time to get some idea of the degree of Coleridge's continuing preoccupation with the phenomena of which these symbols are for him an expression. The fact is that the symbols occur with great fre-

---

[1] *Poems*, pp. 362-68. The standard version of the poem, that of the 1834 edition of the collected poems, will be found in the Appendix.

[2] Marius Bewley, "The Poetry of Coleridge," *Scrutiny*, VIII (March, 1940), 420.

quency in Coleridge's poetry, so that to follow their use in an exhaustive way will necessitate a rather long and perhaps tedious excursion, for which some apology seems appropriate. Its length, if not its tedium, might be justified by the fact that only through noting the universal consistency of their use throughout Coleridge's poetic opus is it possible to appreciate the full force of their use in "Dejection."

This raises a question of critical procedure. The relation between the unity of the individual work of art as a self-contained, unique whole, and the unity which can be glimpsed in the whole opus of a given artist, presents a complex and very delicate problem, so that the interpretation of one poem by means of another can be of very dubious validity. The fact that rosemary symbolizes remembrance in one poem is by no means necessarily relevant to the interpretation of another poem by the same author in which rosemary occurs. But when we find an image occurring throughout a poetic opus, and always with apparently similar force,[3] this fact can serve as a key to interpretation, and is likely to indicate a central preoccupation of the poet. Thus, one of several fruitful ways of reading poetry is to read the opus of the poet as a kind of whole, its units interpreting one another, each one revealing a facet of the whole which is the total consciousness of the poet. It is in this perspective that the following examination is undertaken.

In the earliest instance of the use of the two symbols, a "Sonnet to the Autumnal Moon" (1788),[4] the symbolism is ordinary enough, the moon being associated with Hope, the storm with Despair, and, appropriately for the age of sixteen at which Coleridge wrote this poem, Despair is chased away by Hope. But the

[3] The storm image is employed in several political poems written between 1788 and 1793, but its use in them seems clearly irrelevant to the present inquiry.
[4] *Poems*, p. 5.

genial confusion of the images, producing wonder, is already present:

> Mild Splendour of the various-vested Night!
> Mother of wildly-working visions! Hail!

In "To the Evening Star" (1790?),[5] the atmosphere is again visionary:

> On thee full oft with fixed eye I gaze
> Till I, methinks, all spirit seem to grow.

We shall find that not only moonlight but all half-lights, all reflected, diffused lights, seem to constitute a symbolic cluster for Coleridge.[6] The evening star recurs in "Genevieve" (1791)[7] as "Beauty's light," and in "Anna and Harland" (1791),[8] the story of a maiden killed by grief at her lover's death, the poet says,

> I love to sit upon her tomb's dark grass,
>   Then Memory backward rolls Time's shadowy tide;
>   The tales of other days before me glide:
> With eager thought I seize them as they pass;
> For fair, tho' faint, the forms of Memory gleam,
> Like Heaven's bright beauteous bow reflected in the stream.

In the same short poem, a version of the storm also appears:

> To Death's dark house did grief-worn Anna haste,
>   Yet here her pensive ghost delights to stay;
>   Oft pouring on the winds the broken lay—
> And hark, I hear her—'twas the passing blast.

Here already the storm is a stimulant to the imagination, and the products of the imagination issue from the shadowy tide of memory into the faint gleam of a reflected light.[9]

---

[5] *Ibid.*, pp. 16-17.

[6] Cf. Robert Penn Warren, "A Poem of Pure Imagination," pp. 86 ff., for a full discussion of the use of these symbols in *The Rime of the Ancient Mariner*.

[7] *Poems*, pp. 19-20.

[8] *Ibid.*, p. 16.

[9] One is tempted to see in this inconsiderable little poem, written when Coleridge

Warren points out that the motto from Burnet affixed to *The Rime of the Ancient Mariner* (1797-98) ends: "But meanwhile we must earnestly seek after truth, maintaining measure, that we may distinguish things certain from those uncertain, day from night." "The motto," he continues,

> ends on the day-night contrast, and points to this contrast as a central fact of the poem. We may get some clue to the content of the distinction by remembering that in the poem the good events take place under the aegis of the moon, the bad events under that of the sun. This, it may be objected, reverses the order of Burnet, who obviously wishes to equate the 'certain' or the good with the day and the 'uncertain' or bad with night. Coleridge's reversal is, I take it, quite deliberate—an ironical reversal which, in effect, says that the rational and conventional view expressed by Burnet seeks truth in the wrong light. In other words, Burnet becomes the spokesman of what we shall presently find Coleridge calling the 'mere reflective faculty' which partakes of 'Death.'[10]

The supposition of a deliberate ironical reversal here may be a little far-fetched, especially in view of the content of the whole motto, which suggests other reasons for Coleridge's choice of it; but Warren could have found his theory of the significance of the symbols in question most directly borne out in a poem of the period we are now considering, "Absence" (1791),[11] in which thoughts of "Joy" bring on the two symbols:

> The Sun who ne'er remits his fires
> On heedless eyes may pour the day:
> The Moon, that oft from heaven retires,
> Endears her renovated ray.
> What though she leave the sky unblest

---

was eighteen, an anticipation of Wordsworth's observation that poetry "takes its origin from emotion recollected in tranquility," but perhaps the temptation ought to be resisted.

[10] "A Poem of Pure Imagination," pp. 86-87.

[11] *Poems*, pp. 29-30.

To mourn awhile in murky vest?
When she relumes her lovely light,
We bless the Wanderer of the Night.

The matter-of-fact sun is constant, and so, in a sense, breeds contempt; or rather, the light it sheds on the world, being constant, involves no indication of special privilege. As in this poem "We bless the Wanderer of the Night," so the Mariner was to "bless" the creatures of the night and be saved through doing so. In this poem, written at the age of nineteen, Coleridge has as yet had no serious indication that the moon cannot forever be counted on to "relume her lovely light"—caprice is a grace when we are confident. What is most important here is that the moon is associated with "Joy," which was to become for Coleridge a synonym for the poetic experience.

And so again in "Happiness" (1791),[12] a poem addressed to his brother George, he says:

'Tis thine the converse deep to hold
With all the famous sons of old;
And thine the happy waking dream
While hope pursues some favorite theme,
As oft when Night o'er Heaven is spread,
Round this maternal seat you tread,
Where far from splendour, far from riot,
In silence wrapt sleeps careless Quiet.
'Tis thine with Fancy oft to talk,
And thine the peaceful evening walk;
And what to thee the sweetest are—
The setting sun, the Evening Star—
The tints, which live along the sky,
And moon that meets thy raptur'd eye,
Where oft the tear shall grateful start,
Dear silent pleasures of the heart!

[12] *Ibid.*, p. 32.

It seems safe to assume that Coleridge is here attributing his own reactions to his brother. It is already evident that for Coleridge the moon-world is symbolic not of happiness in the sense of peace and mirth, but of the realm of Imagination, of intimate, melancholy-fruitful contact with something beyond and closely dear, the realm of Vision, of magic. It is relevant to note that although religious faith occupies final place among the elements of happiness reviewed in this poem—the others are the joys of imagination, friendship, and love—it enters in a rather perfunctory way at the end, as applying only to life after death. Poetic communion with Nature occupies central place.

In the lines "Imitated from Ossian" (1793),[13] there is a "restless gale," a "breeze" rather than a storm, in which the lily waves during its brief life, to be sought in vain by the traveler on the morrow.

> With eager gaze and wetted cheek
> 　My wonted haunts along,
> Thus, faithful Maiden! *thou* shalt seek
> 　The Youth of simplest song.

> But I along the breeze shall roll
> 　The voice of feeble power;
> And dwell the Moon-beam of thy soul,
> 　In slumber's nightly hour.

The breeze is here the vehicle by means of which the lover is borne in upon the imagination of the beloved, where he illumes it as a moonbeam. The moonbeam image is an addition of Coleridge's, not suggested by the original of Macpherson. This is likewise the case in "The Complaint of Ninathóma" (1793),[14] also imitated from Ossian:

> A Ghost! by my cavern it darted!
> 　In moon-beams the Spirit was drest—

[13] *Ibid.*, pp. 38-39.
[14] *Ibid.*, pp. 39-40.

> For lovely appear the Departed
>   When they visit the dreams of my rest!
> But disturb'd by the tempest's commotion
>   Fleet the shadowy forms of delight—
> Ah cease, thou shrill blast of the ocean!
>   To howl through my cavern by night.

The breeze, become a tempest, chases away the "forms of delight." We shall find that this ambiguity of the wind image persists throughout the poems and furnishes one of the prime symbolic vehicles of "Dejection."

A poem called "Songs of the Pixies" (1793),[15] conventional enough to include "Evening's dusky car," is ready-made for moon symbolism, and, in keeping with the spirit of the poem, in which the "Ladies" are invited to partake of the festivity, the pixies circle "the Spirit of the Western Gale" as he slumbers. But even into this gentle scene a wilder element is introduced:

> Hence thou lingerer, Light!
> Eve saddens into Night.
> Mother of wildly working dreams! we view
>   The sombre hours, that round thee stand
>   With downcast eyes (a duteous band!)
> Their dark robes dripping with the heavy dew,
>   Sorceress of the ebon throne!
>   Thy power the Pixies own,
>   When round thy raven brow
>   Heaven's lucent roses glow,
>   And clouds in watery colours drest
> Float in light drapery o'er thy sable vest:
> What time the pale moon sheds a softer day
> Mellowing the woods beneath its pensive beam:
> For mid the quivering light 'tis ours to play,
> Aye dancing to the cadence of the stream.[16]

[15] *Ibid.*, pp. 40-44.
[16] *Ibid.*, pp. 43-44.

It is hard to escape the feeling that in this stanza Coleridge is letting himself be carried beyond his immediate theme (the next stanza begins, "Welcome, Ladies!"), with the sadness, the somberness, and the wildly-working dreams. The pale moon mellows the woods beneath its "pensive" beam. The power of night is that of magic, of the pixies, who shun the "blaze of day." And there is even a species of storm:

> When fades the moon to shadowy pale,
> And sends the cloud before the gale.[17]

"The Gentle Look" (1793?) [18] is another evening poem in which the evening-moon image operates as an ambivalent symbol of sadness and joy:

> Thou gentle Look, that didst my soul beguile,
>> Why hast thou left me? Still in some fond dream
> Revisit my sad heart, auspicious Smile!
>> As falls on closing flowers the lunar beam:
> What time in sickly mood, at parting day
>> I lay me down and think of happier years;
> Of joys, that glimmer'd in Hope's twilight ray,
>> Then left me in a darkling vale of tears.

The moonbeam is again, as in the lines "Imitated from Ossian," the symbol of mysterious communion, but the joy associated with the moon-world is already a fragile, evanescent joy.

The poem which, in its first draft, was called "An Effusion at Evening" (1792),[19] and, in its later published version, "Lines on an Autumnal Evening" (1793),[20] was perhaps more aptly titled in the first instance—as an "effusion." It is a kind of wandering reminiscence of youth, and of love, real or imaginary, and it

[17] *Ibid.*, p. 41.
[18] *Ibid.*, pp. 47-48.
[19] *Ibid.*, pp. 49-50.
[20] *Ibid.*, pp. 51-54.

finds room for an epic simile as well as a large number of conventional images. The final version is thirty-eight lines longer than the first draft and includes thirteen lines of which Coleridge says in a note:

I entreat the Public's pardon for having carelessly suffered to be printed such intolerable stuff as this and the following thirteen lines. They have not the merit even of originality: as every thought is to be found in the Greek Epigrams.[21]

It may be assumed that at this point in his life Coleridge knew relatively little about lost love from personal experience. The first draft begins, appropriately enough, "Imagination, Mistress of my Love!" The final version, in addition to its greater length, is distinguished by its somberer tone—it was apparently written not long before the lowest point in Coleridge's early career, his desperate excursion into the cavalry.[22] But the poem is of interest to us here because in both versions the moonlight and the breeze are the agencies through which the mind of the poet is to be kindled to an image of his absent love. The spring of Imagination and Fancy (here equated rather than distinguished) is sought in the two twilights, while the "blameless day" is remembered as a time of peace and mirth, of which the storm is here the destroyer:

> As oft in climes beyond the western Main
> Where boundless spreads the wildly-silent Plain,
> The savage Hunter, who his drowsy frame
> Has bask'd beneath the Sun's unclouded Flame,
> Awakes amid the tempest-troubled air,
> The Thunder's peal and Lightning's lurid glare—
> Aghast he hears the rushing Whirlwind's Sweep,
> And sad recalls the sunny hour of Sleep!
> So lost by storms along Life's wild'ring Way
> Mine eye reverted views that cloudless Day,

[21] *Ibid.*, p. 52*n.*; quoted from the 1796 edition of *Poems*, p. 183.
[22] *Ibid.*, p. 51*n.*

When, ——! on thy banks I joy'd to rove
While Hope with kisses nurs'd the infant Love![23]

A certain richness of paradox is evident here, where the sunny hour is an hour of *sleep,* albeit preferred to a moonless, "lurid" tempest night. Actually by this time Coleridge appears to have built up a consistent scale of symbolic reference involving the three stages of light—full daylight, the various half-lights, and dark night. Sunlight is associated with the normal, even happy everyday world (something like Wordsworth's "light of common day"[24]); dark night with tribulation and despair. Both of these symbolic usages are quite obvious and conventional, though Coleridge's use of them in particular poems is not always so. More peculiar to Coleridge is the association of the half-lights with Vision, with Joy, touched as it so often is by sadness, and with the Imagination, the creative experience. In this view, we may recall, the motto from Burnet affixed to *The Ancient Mariner* need not be accounted for by supposing a deliberate ironical reversal, since it is not night as such that Coleridge opposes to common daylight.[25]

One change from the first draft of "An Effusion" to the final version, "Lines," deserves special attention. The next to last stanza in both versions is an apostrophe to the poet's "native brook," which appears thus in the first draft:

Sweet ——! where Pleasure's streamlet glides
Fann'd by soft winds to curl in mimic tides;
Where Mirth and Peace beguile the blameless Day;
And where Friendship's fixt star beams a mellow'd Ray;[26]

[23] *Ibid.,* p. 50.
[24] An interesting comparison could be made between the symbolic cluster here being considered and the similar but not identical one in Wordsworth's "Ode." Cf. Cleanth Brooks' analysis of the "Ode" in *The Well-Wrought Urn* (New York: Reynal & Hitchcock, 1947), pp. 114-38.
[25] See in this book pp. 70-71.
[26] *Poems,* p. 50.

The corresponding lines in the final version are these:

> Dear native brook! like Peace, so placidly
> Smoothing through fertile fields thy current meek!
> Dear native brook! where first young Poesy
> Stared wildly-eager in her noontide dream![27]

The reference to "young Poesy" introduced in the second version as a substitute for Mirth and Peace has the merit of referring back to the "sunny hour of sleep": *young* poesy's state of mind is that of a "noontide dream." I take the allusion to be affectionately patronizing, and nostalgic. Already, at the age of twenty, Coleridge is looking back on his carefree youth. But the light of noontide had never presided over Coleridge's poetic activity. The last stanza of the poem is the first forecast of "Dejection":

> Scenes of my Hope! the aching eye ye leave
> Like yon bright hues that paint the clouds of eve!
> Tearful and saddening with the sadden'd blaze
> Mine eye the gleam pursues with wistful gaze:
> Sees shades on shades with deeper tint impend,
> Till chill and damp the moonless night descend.[28]

It is a measure of the crucial difference between the states of mind reflected in this poem and in "Dejection," where he watches just such a fading sun, that in the latter case there *is* a moon, and yet no Joy.

In "Lines to a Beautiful Spring in a Village" (1794),[29] noon and moon are used in contrasting but equally favorable ways:

> Life's current then ran sparkling to the noon,
> Or silvery stole beneath the pensive Moon:
> Ah! now it works rude brakes and thorns among,
> Or o'er the rough rocks bursts and foams along!

[27] *Ibid.*, p. 54. The rest of the passage in both versions is a tissue of personifications; the line about "Friendship's fixt star" occurs later in the published version.
[28] *Ibid.*
[29] *Ibid.*, pp. 58-59.

It might be better to accept this as an exception in the development being outlined than to risk slandering Coleridge by pointing out that this is the only time we run into a noon-moon rhyme, and arousing suspicions on that score. The fact is that throughout this poem he is celebrating peaceful, happy village life, and this was not the last time that Coleridge was to think wistfully of the possibility of combining the moon-world and domesticity, even of substituting the latter for the former.[30]

There is such a suggestion in the next poem to be considered, the sonnet "Pantisocracy" (1794).[31] Confidently repressing his "visionary soul," he seeks a "cottag'd dell / Where Virtue calm with careless step may stray," and yet, in the very next lines,

> dancing to the moonlight roundelay,
> The wizard Passions weave a holy spell.

At the end of the poem the new joys he seeks are again bathed in sunlight:

> And see the rising sun, and feel it dart
> New rays of pleasance trembling to the heart.

This sonnet marks the high point in Coleridge's quite vain hope to achieve Joy and "pleasance" together.

In "Elegy" (1794?)[32] moonlight is the spurned lover's element, and it is the gale which brings him into the faithless mistress's imagination—"Still Edmund's voice accused her in each gale."

The sonnet "To the Author of 'The Robbers'" (1794?)[33] is all midnight and tempest. In a note, Coleridge describes the occasion of his reading the play and its impact upon him. "A Winter midnight—the wind high—and 'The Robbers' for the first time!— The readers will conceive what I felt."[34]

---

30 See in this book pp. 34 ff.
31 *Poems*, pp. 68-69.
32 *Ibid.*, pp. 69-70.
33 *Ibid.*, pp. 72-73.
34 *Ibid.*, pp. 72-73n.

Ah! Bard tremendous in sublimity!
Could I behold thee in thy loftier mood
Wandering at eve with finely-frenzied eye
Beneath some vast old tempest-swinging wood!
Awhile with mute eye gazing I would brood:
Then weep aloud in a wild ecstasy.

His comment on the play in the same note is a good indication of what he thought was to be achieved by the introduction of the supernatural into poetry: "Schiller introduces no supernatural beings; yet his human beings agitate and astonish more than all the *goblin* rout—even of Shakespeare." (He later suppressed this note, possibly as a result of the introduction of a "goblin rout" in *The Ancient Mariner*.) "Agitate" is the more interesting word here—the tempest is the symbol of that agitation, that deep stirring, of that feeling of union, hence Joy, with which Coleridge identifies the poetic experience.

The two versions of the sonnet "To the Rev. W. L. Bowles" (1794-96) [35] offer some instructive variations on the theme being considered. The first five lines of the first version read thus:

My heart has thank'd thee, BOWLES! for those soft strains,
    That, on the still air floating, tremblingly
    Wak'd in me Fancy, Love, and Sympathy!
For hence, not callous to a Brother's pains
Thro' Youth's gay prime and thornless paths I went;

In the second version these lines become:

My heart has thank'd thee, BOWLES! for those soft strains
    Whose sadness soothes me, like the murmuring
    Of wild-bees in the sunny showers of spring!
For hence not callous to the mourner's pains
Through Youth's gay prime and thornless paths I went:

The explicit note of sadness is added, even for the period of youth, and for the three important abstractions, Fancy, Love, and Sym-

[35] *Ibid.*, pp. 84-85.

pathy, wild-bees in the sunny showers of spring have been substituted. The very next line of the first version, "And when the *darker* day of life began," would carry on the sun metaphor introduced in the second version, but this line is itself replaced in the second version, and the sonnet continues:

> And when the mightier Throes of mind began,
>   And drove me forth a thought-bewildered man,
> Their mild and manliest melancholy lent
> A mingled charm, such as the pang consign'd
>   To slumber, though the big tear it renew'd;
>   Bidding a strange mysterious PLEASURE brood
> Over the wavy and tumultuous mind,

The three abstractions, considered not in their sunny youthful awakening but in their mature realization, are all taken care of in the "strange mysterious PLEASURE" (in the former version a "shadowy" pleasure, albeit with "mysterious wings"); and the sunlight-darkness opposition is completed by the final couplet, nearly identical in the two versions:

> As the great SPIRIT erst with plastic sweep
> Mov'd on the darkness of the unform'd deep.

In the later version the spirit of poetry, even in youth, is characterized by a note of sadness, "soothing" sadness. The awakening of Fancy, Love, and Sympathy is less important to be dwelt upon than the contrast between their sunny aspect in youth and their mightier throes in maturity. The metaphorical "darker day" is discarded for its more direct equivalent, "the mightier Throes of mind"—possibly the paradox which would have been created by retaining it in the same version with the "sunny showers of spring" seemed too facile. In both versions this spirit of poetry enables him to envelop the darker day, the throes of mind, into PLEASURE (here a two-syllabled word for Joy), but it is a pleasure

described by means of the most solemn of similes, likened to the
Holy Spirit brooding upon the waters of chaos, the most exalted
archetype of the creative spirit. In such throes, how could one
regret the sunny showers of spring?

The sonnet "To Robert Southey" (1795) [36] is really a third
version of the original sonnet to Bowles, beginning:

> SOUTHEY! thy melodies steal o'er mine ear
> Iike far-off joyance, or the murmuring
> Of wild bees in the sunny showers of Spring—
> Sounds of such mingled import as may cheer

> The lonely breast, yet rouse a mindful tear:

Here poetry, when likened to the murmuring of wild bees in the
sunny showers of spring, serves to temper joy with sadness, and
in doing so awakens "Hope-born FANCY," under whose "rich
showers of dewy fragrance" "PASSION's drooping Myrtles sear /
Blossom anew!" The contrast is no longer between the effects of
the same poetry in the reader's youth and maturity, but between
the effects of different strains of poetry. The joyful strain arouses
a tear and so awakens Fancy. The sadder and more thrilling strain
evokes past Delight and the tearful gleam of Pleasure. The whole
poem is in a lower, more constant, and more delicate key of contrast than the sonnets to Bowles. Perhaps because the image of the
Holy Spirit seemed less appropriate in connection with Southey
than with Bowles, the great Spirit who "with plastic sweep /
Mov'd on the darkness of the unform'd deep" gives place at the
end to "The imag'd Rainbow on a willowy stream," still another
form of half-light, and that seen in reflection.

In "Lines to a Friend in Answer to a Melancholy Letter"
(1795?),[37] though the storm is employed in a thoroughly conventional way, the peculiar Coleridgean ambiguity slips in:

[36] *Ibid.*, p. 87.
[37] *Ibid.*, p. 90.

Yon setting sun flashes in mournful gleam
Behind those broken clouds, his stormy train:
Tomorrow shall the many-colour'd main
In brightness roll beneath his orient beam!

Wild, as autumnal gust, the hand of Time
Flies o'er his mystic lyre: in shadowy dance
The alternate groups of Joy and Grief advance
Responsive to his varying strains sublime!

The mournful gleam foretokens brightness. Here is another piece of folk meteorology, similar to that found in the stanza from "Sir Patrick Spence" that prefaces "Dejection." There is a bit of doggerel that goes:

Red in the morning,
Sailors take warning;
Red at night,
Sailors delight.

But in this poem Grief and Joy, the mournful gleam and the orient beam, are caught up together in a shadowy dance, both equally touched by the sublimity of the strains that issue from Time's "mystic lyre." In this poem Coleridge is offering his friend some familiar necessitarian doctrine as a cure for melancholy. In later stanzas Fate and Fortune take the place of Time. But in the second of the stanzas quoted there is something more complicated than the simple alternation between grief and joy, governed by necessity. The hand of time, which produces such an ordered, if shadowy, dance, is "wild," wild as the autumnal gust, and it sweeps a "mystic lyre." One is reminded of the winds that sweep Coleridge's Eolian Harp, in the poem of that name and in "Dejection." They are the winds of poetic inspiration, wild and unpredictable, yet producing order when the poet is able to respond to them. But the order they can be counted on to produce is produced in the *poem,* not in the life of the poet. It was Coleridge's

faith in the latter function of the poetic experience of nature, indirectly reflected here, which was to be his undoing and was to
issue in "Dejection."

It is quite natural that the nightingale should be seen in moonlight, and become the symbol of poetic creation, the "Minstrel of
the Moon":

> Sister of love-lorn Poets, Philomel! . . . .
> How many wretched Bards address *thy* name,
> And hers, that full-orb'd Queen that shines above.
> But I *do* hear thee, and the high bough mark,
> Within whose mild moon-mellow'd foliage hid
> Thou warblest sad thy pity-pleading strains.
> O! I have listen'd, till my working soul,
> Waked by those strains to thousand phantasies,
> Absorb'd hath ceased to listen![38]

But, he goes on, 'all thy soft diversities of tone . . .

> Are not so sweet as is the voice of her,
> My Sara—best-beloved of human kind!
> When breathing the pure soul of tenderness,
> She thrills me with the Husband's promis'd name!'

The comparison between love and poetry, in favor of the former,
might be put down simply to the enthusiasm of the anticipating
lover; but we recall "Happiness," written in 1791, in which he
was already looking forward to love as an ultimate fulfillment.
It would almost seem, viewed in terms of the symbols we are
following through the poems, that Coleridge looked to consummated love to deliver him from the storm of poetry, to rescue
him from the moon-world. It must be remembered that the love
under consideration here is his love for Sara Fricker, which, unlike the love he felt for Sara Hutchinson, seems never to have
been threatening in its own right.

[38] *Poems,* pp. 93-94, "To the Nightingale" (1795).

In "Lines Written at Shurton Bars" (1795)[39] the opposition
between the moon-world and domestic love is most explicitly
stated:

> Nor travels my meandering eye
> The starry wilderness on high;
>   Nor now with curious sight
> I mark the glow-worm as I pass,
> Move with 'green radiance' through the grass,
>   An emerald light.
>
> O ever present to my view!
> My wafted spirit is with you,[40]

And further on:

> But why with sable wand unblessed
> Should Fancy rouse within my breast
>   Dim-visag'd shapes of Dread?
> Untenanting its beauteous clay
> My Sara's soul has wing'd its way,
>   And hovers round my head![41]

Fancy, which surely belongs to the "starry wilderness," the realm
of poetic experience, is an unblessed, unwelcome intrusion. A
major portion of the poem is taken up with exorcising it:

> When slowly sank the day's last gleam:
>   You rous'd each gentler sense,
> As sighing o'er the Blossom's bloom
> Meek Evening wakes its soft perfume
>   With viewless influence.
>
> And hark, my Love! The sea-breeze moans
> Through yon reft house! O'er rolling stones
>   In bold ambitious sweep
> The onward-surging tides supply
> The silence of the cloudless sky
>   With mimic thunders deep.

---

[39] *Ibid.*, pp. 96-100.
[40] *Ibid.*, p. 97.
[41] *Ibid.*

Dark reddening from the channell'd Isle
(Where stands one solitary pile
  Unslated by the blast)
The Watchfire, like a sullen star
Twinkles to many a dozing Tar
  Rude cradled on the mast.

Even there—beneath that light-house tower—
In the tumultuous evil hour
  Ere Peace with Sara came,
Time was I should have thought it sweet
To count the echoings of my feet,
  And watch the storm-vex'd flame.

And there in black soul-jaundic'd fit
A sad gloom-pamper'd Man to sit,
  And listen to the roar:
When mountain surges bellowing deep
With an uncouth monster leap
  Plung'd foaming on the shore.[42]

But Sara arouses "each gentler sense," as opposed to the "bold ambitious sweep" of the tides. He recalls the pleasures of the storm,
"ere Peace with Sara came," and dismisses them almost with disdain. One is inclined to ask whether it was a "gloom-pamper'd
Man" who would "weep aloud in a wild ecstasy" could he but see
Schiller wandering "Beneath some vast old tempest-swinging
wood!"[43]

But Fancy now more gaily sings;
Or if awhile she droop her wings,
  As skylarks mid the corn,
On summer fields she grounds her breast:
The oblivious poppy o'er her nest
  Nods till returning morn.

[42] *Ibid.*, p. 98.
[43] See in this book pp. 78-79.

Still the other symbol intrudes, only to be exorcised again:

> When stormy Midnight howling round
> Beats on our roof with clattering sound,
>   To me your arms you'll stretch:
> Great God! you'll say—To us be kind
> O shelter from this loud bleak wind
>   The homeless, friendless wretch![44]

This same opposition between the storm of imagination and domestic peace furnishes the framework of "The Eolian Harp" (1795).[45] It seems to be less often noted that the poem begins with Sara (a "pensive" Sara) than that she enters at the end to rebuke Coleridge for unhallowed thoughts.

> My pensive Sara! thy soft cheek reclin'd
> Thus on my arm, most soothing sweet it is
> To sit beside our Cot, our Cot o'ergrown
> With the white-flower'd Jasmin, and the broad-leav'd Myrtle,
> (Meet emblems they of Innocence and Love!)

He finds himself actually installed in "the cottag'd dell / Where Virtue calm with careless step may stray," of which he had dreamed in "Pantisocracy," without having had to make the voyage to America, and within the framework of no visionary political system. There, in addition, "dancing to the moonlight roundelay, / The wizard Passions" were to "weave a holy spell." And surely enough they do. He and Sara

> watch the clouds, that late were rich with light,
> Slow saddening round, and mark the star of eve
> Serenely brilliant (such should Wisdom be)
> Shine opposite! How exquisite the scents
> Snatch'd from yon bean-field! and the world *so* hushed!
> The still murmur of the distant Sea
> Tells us of silence.

[44] *Poems*, pp. 98-99.
[45] *Ibid.*, pp. 100-2.

> And that simplest Lute,
> Placed lengthwise in the clasping casement, hark!
> How by the desultory breeze caress'd,
> Like some coy maid half yielding to her lover,
> It pours such sweet upbraiding, as must needs
> Tempt to repeat the wrong! And now, its strings
> Boldlier swept, the long sequacious notes
> Over delicious surges sink and rise,
> Such a soft floating witchery of sound
> As twilight Elfins make, when they at eve
> Voyage on gentle gales from Fairy-Land,
> Where melodies round honey-dropping flowers,
> Footless and wild, like birds of Paradise,
> Nor pause, nor perch, hovering on untam'd wing![46]

This is the same lute that seven years later was to be swept by an "agony of torture" in "Dejection," and to which in 1808, he was to compare his "whole frame," under the "perpetual touch and sweet pressure" of love, a love so different from that offered by Sara. And is this desultory breeze quite different from the sea-breeze that moaned through yon reft house in "Lines at Shurton Bars," and that was shorn of its power when "Peace with Sara came"? Is it, despite the delicate elfin imagery, quite different from the "plastic sweep" that "Mov'd on the darkness of the un-form'd deep," the harbinger of Pleasure to "the wavy and tu-multuous mind" in the sonnet to Bowles?[47] Here are the lines it engenders:

> O! the one Life within us and abroad,
> Which meets all motion and becomes its soul,
> A light in sound, a sound-like power in light,
> Rhythm in all thought, and joyance everywhere—
> Methinks, it should have been impossible
> Not to love all things in a world so fill'd;

---

[46] *Ibid.*, pp. 100-1.
[47] See in this book pp. 79-81.

> Where the breeze warbles, and the mute still air
> Is Music slumbering on her instrument.[48]

Here, as later in "Dejection," the two symbols coalesce—"A light in sound, a sound-like power in light"—and produce a kind of apotheosis, embracing all things in love and "joyance."[49] This passage is of great interest for the study of Coleridge's philosophical development,[50] but, engendered by the breeze, the lines also mark a stage in his poetic development. They reveal most explicitly the religious, the essentially mystical nature of what he was looking to the poetic experience for. The passage is significant artistically or theologically as one wishes, because at this stage the two areas were almost indistinguishable for Coleridge. He felt himself about to achieve mystical union through the poetic experience:

> And what if all of animated nature
> Be but organic Harps diversely fram'd,
> That tremble into thought, as o'er them sweeps
> Plastic and vast, one intellectual breeze,
> At once the soul of each, and God of all?[51]

It is indeed the same "plastic sweep" encountered in the sonnets to Bowles, Coleridge's life-time preoccupation. Is Coleridge here falling into a kind of pantheism? It seems quite clear that he is, and the repudiation of it will be made at the price of very nearly killing poetry in him.

Coleridge never seems to have been tempted, like Mallarmé, for instance, along the occult, magical by-road of poetry, where, through his "shaping mind," the poet seeks to *avail* himself of

---

48 *Poems*, p. 101.
49 See comments on "Lines to a Friend," pp. 81-83 in this book.
50 See Gingerich, "From Necessity to Transcendentalism"; Richards, *Coleridge on Imagination* (New York: Norton, 1950), pp. 148 ff.; Warren, "A Poem of Pure Imagination," pp. 79, 127 (n. 63).
51 *Poems*, p. 102.

the power with which he feels he has come in contact through the poetic experience of the world, in order to use it for his own ends, although he may be describing something like the magical use of art in "Kubla Khan"—Kubla "decrees" his pleasure-dome, creates a world through the power of the word, and the speaker in the poem, if he could imitate him, would be banned as a necromancer. The fact is that he cannot. But when that does not happen, the other by-road is still open: to become pure instrument, like the passive Eolian harp, and *thus* be identified with the universal power. Magic or pantheism, these are two roads open to those who confuse the poetic and the mystical ways.[52]

But as we have noticed before, in the build-up of his romance with Sara Fricker as it is reflected in the poems, particularly in terms of the sun-moon-storm complex, Coleridge seems to be flying into domestic contentment to *escape* the throes of the storm of Imagination (at the same time, of course, he is making a virtue of what he conceived to be necessity). And so, as Sara has recalled him from beneath the light-house tower, from the soul-jaundic'd fit of a gloom-pamper'd man, from poetry become painful and dangerous to a deeply religious man, it is Sara's image that recalls him from the specific religious heresy into which his poetic spirit is leading him here. But by the same token she recalls him from the kind of mystical experience with which it is here confused in his mind, and invites him to be content with what is, after all, a domesticated deity:

> But thy more serious eye a mild reproof
> Darts, O belovéd Woman! nor such thoughts
> Dim and unhallow'd dost thou not reject,
> Meek daughter in the family of Christ!
> Well hast thou said and holily disprais'd
> These shapings of the unregenerate mind;

[52] See Raïssa Maritain, "Magic, Poetry, and Mysticism," *Situation of Poetry*, pp. 23-36.

> Bubbles that glitter as they rise and break
> On vain Philosophy's aye-babbling spring.
> For never guiltless may I speak of him,
> The Incomprehensible! save when with awe
> I praise him, and with Faith that inly *feels;*
> Who with his saving mercies healèd me,
> A sinful and most miserable man,
> Wilder'd and dark, and gave me to possess
> Peace, and this Cot, and thee, heart-honour'd Maid![53]

Coleridge is trying here, at the age of twenty-three, to adopt the attitude reflected in Milton's phrase, "Vain wisdom all, and false philosophy," and the later one in which Milton speaks of the accumulation of classical learning as being like children gathering pebbles on the shore. But the real humility possible to Coleridge at this moment of his life lay on the other side, not on this side of a crucial religious experience, which alone could "heal" him. Looking forward to "Dejection," the last four lines of this poem seem cruelly pathetic.

It is permissible to think that Coleridge was hard put when the moment came to write a poetic appreciation of Joseph Cottle's poems,[54] which present a classic case of the patron turned poet. In the original version he dispenses himself at the very beginning of any obligation to flatter:

> Unboastful Bard! whose verse concise yet clear
> Tunes to smooth melody unconquer'd sense,
> May your fame fadeless live,

(A year later, the "Unboastful Bard" became "My honor'd friend" —more diplomatic but no less guarded.) And then, after referring to "Your modest verse," he proceeds to give a lesson on the stages of poetry:

[53] *Poems,* p. 102.
[54] "To the Author of Poems" (1795), *ibid.,* pp. 102-4.

Circling the base of the Poetic mount
A stream there is, which rolls in lazy flow
Its coal-black waters from Oblivion's fount:
The vapour-poisoned Birds, that fly too low,
Fall with dead swoop, and to the bottom go.
Escaped that heavy stream on pinion fleet
Beneath the Mountain's lofty-frowning brow,
Ere aught of perilous ascent you meet,
A mead of mildest charm delays th' unlabouring feet.

Not there the cloud-clim'd rock, sublime and vast,
That like some giant kind, o'er-glooms the hill;
Nor there the Pine-grove to the midnight blast
Makes solemn music! But th' unceasing rill
To the soft Wren or Lark's descending trill
Murmurs sweet undersong 'mid jasmin flowers.
In this same pleasant meadow, at your will
I ween, you wander'd—there collecting flowers
Of sober tint, and herbs of med'cinable powers!

There for the monarch-murder'd Soldier's tomb
You wove th' unfinish'd wreath of saddest hues;
And to that holier chaplet added bloom
Besprinkling it with Jordan's cleansing dews.
But lo your Henderson awakes the Muse—
His Spirit beckon'd from the mountain's height!
You left the plain and soar'd mid richer views!
So Nature mourn'd when sunk the First Day's light,
With stars, unseen before, spangling her robe of night!

Still soar, my Friend, those richer views among,
Strong, rapid, fervent, flashing Fancy's beam!
Virtue and Truth shall love your gentler song;
But Poesy demands th' impassion'd theme:
Waked by Heaven's silent dews at Eve's mild gleam
With balmy sweets Pomona breathes around!
But if the vext air rush a stormy stream
Or Autumn's shrill gust moan in plaintive sound,
With fruits and flowers she loads the tempest-honor'd ground.[55]

55 *Poems*, pp. 103-4.

This is at least as useful as most definitions of poetic genres. Coleridge had already long since heard Autumn's shrill gust moan, and before the time of "Dejection" he was to find some fruits and flowers upon the tempest-honor'd ground. But his description of that terrain is fraught with the danger he found there, on the cloud-clim'd rock, sublime and vast, where the Pine-grove to the midnight blast makes solemn music. The lower order of poetry is sufficient to embower him "from Noon's sultry influence." The upper-middle order is placed in starlight, at "Eve's mild gleam." But the ultimate fruits and flowers are reaped in the tempest, where danger lies.

The images we have been tracing are not prominent, as one might expect them to be, in the "Monody on the Death of Chatterton."[56] Coleridge concentrates on the external pressures that led up to Chatterton's suicide, rather than upon any inward struggles. The poem was begun very early—in his thirteenth year, according to Coleridge[57]—and added to and subtracted from in the various editions it went through during his lifetime. It is in a section belonging to the period we are now considering (*c.* 1795) that we find the half-lights introduced:

> Ye woods! that wave o'er Avon's rocky steep,
> To Fancy's ear sweet is your murmuring deep!
> For here she loves the cypress wreath to weave;
> Watching with wistful eye, the saddening tints of eve.
> Here, far from men, amid this pathless grove,
> In solemn thought the Minstrel wont to rove,
> Like star-beam on the slow sequester'd tide
> Lone-glittering, through the high tree branching wide.
> And here in Inspiration's eager hour,
> When most the big soul feels the mastering power,
>   These wilds, these caverns roaming o'er,
>   Round which the screaming sea-gulls soar,

[56] *Ibid.*, pp. 125-31.
[57] *Ibid.*, pp. 125-26*n.*

> With wild unequal steps he pass'd along,
> Oft pouring on the winds a broken song:
> Anon, upon some rough rock's fearful brow
> Would pause abrupt—and gaze upon the waves below.[58]

The murmuring breeze, the saddening tints of eve, and the "star-beam on the slow sequester'd tide / Lone-glittering" form the atmosphere of "Inspiration's eager hour, / When most the big soul feels the mastering power." In 1794, when this stanza was the conclusion of the "Monody," and in subsequent editions up to that of 1834, the word "mad'ning" was used instead of "mastering," an echo of Aristotle perhaps, but also, it would seem, more directly to the point in Chatterton's case, as well, in a different sense, as in Coleridge's own.

"To a Young Friend, on His Proposing to Domesticate with the Author" (1796),[59] unlike the poem to Cottle, offers an idyllic, even jovial picture of the poetic life—the setting is

> A mount, not wearisome and bare and steep,
> But a green mountain variously up-piled.

Yet there is throughout the poem a careful balance between the gladsome and the melancholy, and, though the action takes place in full daylight, the idea is "to cheat our noons" under

> That shadowing Pine . . .
> Which latest shall detain the enamour'd sight
> Seen from below, when eve the valley dims,
> Tinged yellow with the rich departing light;

So the half-lights are brought in, if only in prospect, when the poetic experience is in question. The two poets will be

> from the stirring world up-lifted high
> (whose noises, faintly wafted on the wind,

[58] *Ibid.*, pp. 129-30.
[59] *Ibid.*, pp. 155-57.

> To quiet musing shall attune the mind,
> And oft the melancholy *theme* supply) . . . .

Writing in a different mood "To a Friend [Charles Lamb] Who Had Declared His Intention to Write No More Poetry" (1796),[60] he invokes the same tree, this time in storm:

> On a bleak rock, midway the Aonian mount,
> There stands a lone and melancholy tree,
> Whose agéd branches to the midnight blast
> Make solemn music: pluck its darkest bough,
> Ere yet the unwholesome night-dew be exhaled,
> And weeping wreath it round thy Poet's tomb.

In sending a sheaf of poems to his brother George in 1797, Coleridge refers briefly to his hours of poetic inspiration, at the end of a stanza devoted to the perils of friendship and the joys of domesticity, employing the affected double negative which is not infrequent in his early verse:

>   not unhearing
> Of that divine and nightly-whispering Voice
> Which from my childhood to maturer years
> Spake to me of predestinated wreaths,
> Bright with no fading colours![61]

The tempest enters:

> Nor dost thou not sometimes recall those hours,
> When with the joy of hope thou gavest thine ear
> To my wild firstling-lays. Since then my song
> Hath sounded deeper notes, such as beseem
> Or that sad wisdom folly leaves behind,
> Or such as, tuned to these tumultous times,
> Cope with the tempest's swell!

---

[60] *Ibid.*, pp. 158-59.
[61] *Poems*, pp. 173-75, "To the Rev. George Coleridge."

But here it is probable that a political tempest is in question.

Lawrence Hanson singles out "This Lime-Tree Bower My Prison" (1797)[62] as heralding a new stage in Coleridge's poetic development, a

foretaste, of what was to be expected when Coleridge freed himself from the shackles of the Augustan idiom and outlook on nature he had so long despised. Abstractions, at times exquisitely expressed, begin to give place to minute descriptions of nature not less beautifully phrased, which could have come only from one who had discovered the pleasures in detailed observation of the outside world.[63]

This appraisal is certainly justified, especially when we compare the poem with those immediately preceding it, which fairly bristle with personified Innocence, Virtue, Melancholy, and meek Quietness; but minute and accurate though they be, the nature descriptions in this poem show evidence also of careful selection according to a symbolic principle. The roaring dell in which he imagines his friends to be wandering is "only speckled by the mid-day sun," and when it comes to imagining for Lamb a poetic experience of nature, the light is familiar:

> Ah! slowly sink
> Behind the western ridge, thou glorious Sun!
> Shine in the slant beams of the sinking orb,
> Ye purple heath-flowers! richlier burn, ye clouds!
> And kindle, thou blue Ocean! So my friend
> Struck with deep joy may stand, as I have stood,
> Silent with swimming sense; yea gazing round
> On the wide landscape, gaze till all doth seem
> Less gross than bodily; and of such hues
> As veil the Almighty Spirit, when yet he makes
> Spirits perceive his presence.[64]

[62] *Ibid.*, pp. 178-81.
[63] *Life*, p. 159.
[64] *Poems*, pp. 179-80. For comparable statements concerning the experience of love, see in this book pp. 26-27 and pp. 30-31.

And likewise under the lime-tree where he is waiting for their
return, the light is dappled:

> Pale beneath the blaze
> Hung the transparent foliage; and I watch'd
> Some broad and sunny leaf, and lov'd to see
> The shadow of the leaf and stem above
> Dappling its sunshine! And that walnut-tree
> Was richly ting'd, and a deep radiance lay
> Full on the ancient ivy, which usurps
> Those fronting elms, and now, with blackest mass
> Makes their dark branches gleam a lighter hue
> Through the late twilight. . . .[65]

In this atmosphere he feels thoroughly confident concerning the
contact with nature out of whose reverberations poetry grows,
and which is scarcely distinguished from mystical contact with
God.

> Henceforth I shall know
> That Nature ne'er deserts the wise and pure;
> No plot so narrow, be but Nature there,
> No waste so vacant, but may well employ
> Each faculty of sense, and keep the heart
> Awake to Love and Beauty![66]

"France: An Ode" (1798)[67] is primarily a political poem, but its
opening stanza is a good illustration of the intertwining of Coleridge's various interests—politics, philosophy, poetry, religion:

> Ye Clouds! that far above me float and pause,
>   Whose pathless march no mortal may controul!
> Ye Ocean-Waves! that, wheresoe'er ye roll,
> Yield homage only to eternal laws!
> Ye Woods! that listen to the night-birds singing,
>   Midway the smooth and perilous slope reclined,

[65] *Poems,* pp. 180-81.
[66] *Ibid.,* p. 181.
[67] *Ibid.,* pp. 243-47.

Save when your own imperious branches swinging,
  Have made a solemn music of the wind!
Where, like a man beloved of God,
Through glooms, which never woodman trod,
  How oft, pursuing fancies holy,
My moonlight way o'er flowering weeds I wound,
  Inspired beyond the guess of folly,
By each rude shape and wild unconquerable sound!
O ye loud Waves! and O ye Forests high!
  And O ye Clouds that far above me soared!
Thou rising Sun! thou blue rejoicing Sky!
  Yea, every thing that is and will be free!
  Bear witness for me, whereso'er ye be,
  With what deep worship I have still adored
    The spirit of divinest Liberty.[68]

The whole stanza is a kind of religious paean to nature, with explicit necessitarian overtones. The wind and the moonlight are not among the objects apostrophized as symbols of liberty (here, as usual, the sun is the symbol of liberty), but rather they furnish the atmosphere of the scene, and are associated with singing, with "solemn music," "fancies holy," and inspiration. The stanza can be read as another version of the "poetic mount."

"Fears in Solitude" (1798) [69] is another political poem, which, like "France: An Ode," begins with an apostrophe to nature as restorative and as the source of inspiration, as the source of a "meditative joy" which finds "religious meanings in the forms of Nature"; and, as usual, Coleridge describes the light, this time by means of a very delicate and precisely observed comparison. The poet finds himself in a "green and silent spot," a dell "bathed by the mist," as fresh and delicate as

[68] *Ibid.*, pp. 243-44.
[69] *Ibid.*, pp. 256-63.

> the unripe flax
> When, through its half-transparent stalks, at eve,
> The level sunshine glimmers with green light.[70]

"Oh! 'tis a quiet spirit-healing nook!" he continues, and the influences which engender the meditative joy are the song of the lark, the green half-sunlight, and "the breezy air."

The lighting of "The Nightingale" (1798)[71] is ambiguous in terms of the oppositions we have been tracing. The poem begins by expressly remarking the absence of any of those "reliques of the sunken day" which color so many of Coleridge's poems.[72] He says,

> No cloud, no relique of the sunken day
> Distinguishes the West, no long thin slip
> Of sullen light, no obscure trembling hues.[73]

The only light is furnished by the "glimmer of the stream,"

> and though the stars be dim,
> Yet let us think upon the vernal showers
> That gladden the green earth, and we shall find
> A pleasure in the dimness of the stars.[74]

In order for the half-light to be enjoyed, it is necessary to think of daylight (though not a full daylight, even so). The fact seems to be that here for once Coleridge is dealing explicitly with the circumstance that in conventional symbolism day is a happy, favorable symbol and night a sad, unfavorable one,[75] and that the half-lights have no status as symbols of Joy or creativity. And so

---

[70] *Ibid.*, p. 257.

[71] *Ibid.*, pp. 264-67.

[72] See "An Effusion at Evening," lines 3-4, 64-65; "Lines to a Friend," lines 5-6; "The Eolian Harp," lines 6-7; "Monody on the Death of Chatterton," line 117; "To a Young Friend," line 35; "This Lime-Tree Bower," lines 35-36.

[73] *Poems*, p. 264.

[74] *Ibid.*

[75] See Warren's remarks on the Burnet motto affixed to *The Ancient Mariner*, p. 70 in this book.

he singles out a daytime half-light that does seem to be a naturally joyful one, "the vernal showers of Spring," found in the sonnets to Bowles and Southey, and to this he likens the absolute minimum of light existing in this scene, the reflection of dim stars in the stream. There is already an underlying appeal here to the oneness of nature as the source of joy. Perhaps in this poem he is more than usually conscious of the paradoxical element in his customary symbolic use of dim lights because he is about to go counter to an even more firmly entrenched conventional symbol, that of the nightingale as a melancholy bird. He quotes Milton's line, "Most musical, most melancholy," and continues:

> A melancholy bird? Oh! idle thought!
> In Nature there is nothing melancholy.[76]

He explains the conventional usage as an instance of the pathetic fallacy, a case of someone's reading his own personal sorrow into nature. And the poet, he goes on, overconcerned with the art, the technique of poetry, with "building up the rhyme," simply echoes the conceit,

> When he had better far have stretched his limbs
> Beside a brook in mossy forest-dell,
> By sun or moonlight, to the influxes
> Of shapes and sounds and shifting elements
> Surrendering his whole spirit, of his song
> And of his fame forgetful! so his fame
> Should share in Nature's immortality,
> A venerable thing! and so his song
> Should make all Nature lovelier, and itself
> Be loved like Nature![77]

[76] *Poems*, p. 264.
[77] *Ibid.*, p. 265. In the same year in which this poem was written we find Goethe speaking of the artist's "penetrating into the object as well as into depths of his own spirit, and of producing in his works not merely something which is easily and superficially effective, but in rivalry with nature, something spiritually-organic, and of giving his work such a content and form that it will seem at

When one has learned to do this, as he and Wordsworth and Dorothy had, "Nature's sweet voices" are "always full of love and joyance!"—the nightingale is a merry bird.

This poem represents the high point of Coleridge's unqualified faith in the poetic experience as a completely fulfilling contact with Nature, a nature conceived as a positive, unmixed good, with which one is united, in which one is absorbed, completely forgetful of self. One has only to leave oneself open to its "influxes," as the mystic leaves himself open to divine grace. There is even the note of asceticism, orthodoxly conceived as preparing the soul in a negative way, removing impediments to the reception of what is a completely gratuitous gift. In this case the asceticism consists in avoiding artificial amusements ("ball-rooms and hot theatres") and artificial sentiments, in favor of contact with nature. Then all aspects of nature produce joy, and it is only our own weaknesses that may result in the introduction of an element of sadness. Coleridge himself was most susceptible to these influxes under certain circumstances—in certain lights and weathers, for example—but he is saying here that this is accidental, that the experience may occur "by sun or moon-light."

What is most important to note is the distinction Coleridge is making between the *poetic experience* of nature, and its artistic elaboration in an actual work of art. He is in fact inveighing, quite properly from any point of view, against the kind of artistic elaboration which proceeds without the basis of a previous poetic experience, and is therefore pure fabrication, and falsification. Explicit consciousness of this valid distinction between "poetic experience" and "art" was a relatively new development among poets, may even be said to be a contribution of the ro-

---

once natural and above nature." Quoted by Meyer Abrams, *The Mirror and the Lamp* (New York: W. W. Norton & Co., 1958), p. 206.

mantics.[78] Having made the distinction explicitly, having discovered the poetic experience as such, in its pure state as it were,
their danger was that of detaching it from its natural end, which
is precisely artistic elaboration, the making of a work, *poiesis*.
Once detached and exalted as the romantics exalted it, once made
an end in itself, the poetic experience is easily confused with the
properly mystical experience, and is expected to produce a comparable fulfillment. The inevitable resulting disappointment issues in the silence of Rimbaud, or Coleridge's dejection.

In "The Nightingale," after resolving the night-day paradox
by saying in effect, in the little homily quoted, that given the
right disposition on the part of the subject, sunlight and moonlight, the ordinary and the mysterious, are equally capable of
inducing the poetic experience, Coleridge plunges into his own
accustomed moon-lit world, describing a scene that contains a
number of elements reminiscent of "Kubla Khan," a grove, wild
with tangled underwood, "hard by a castle huge," where nightingales are

> Stirring the air with such a harmony,
> That should you close your eyes, you might almost
> Forget it was not day! On moonlight bushes,
> Whose dewy leaflets are but half-disclosed,
> You may perchance behold them on the twigs,
> Their bright, bright eyes, their eyes both bright and full,
> Glistening, while many a glow-worm in the shade
> Lights up her love-torch.[79]

And finally there is a maid, who wanders in the castle garden

> (Even like a Lady vowed and dedicate
> To something more than Nature in the grove) ....[80]

[78] See Jacques Maritain, *Situation of Poetry*, pp. 37-44. See in this book pp. 157
ff; and Abrams, *The Mirror and the Lamp*, p. 3 and *passim*.
[79] *Poems*, pp. 265-66.
[80] *Ibid.*, p. 266.

To her demon-lover, perhaps. The music is controlled by the moon, and when the moon appears from behind a cloud the nightingales burst forth,

> As if some sudden gale had swept at once
> A hundred airy harps![81]

Here again is the gale that swept "The Eolian Harp," producing "Such a soft floating witchery of sound," that a little "Kubla Khan" was almost created on the spot;[82] and it is the gale that "moans and rakes / Upon the strings of this Eolian lute, / Which better far were mute," by the time of "Dejection."

The poem ends with a touching little story, "a father's tale," about Coleridge's infant son, Hartley, whom Coleridge took out into the moonlight when he cried (thereby going against all superstitions concerning the maddening effect of moonlight, be it noted):

> And he beheld the moon, and, hushed at once,
> Suspends his sobs, and laughs most silently,
> While his fair eyes, that swam with undropped tears,
> Did glitter in the yellow moon-beam![83]

We are reminded of the glittering eyes of Geraldine in *Christabel,* and the eyes of the sailors in *The Ancient Mariner,* and the "flashing eyes" in "Kubla Khan." The ambiguity is rich, both within this passage (the innocent babe who laughs with "glittering" eyes), and between this passage and the others referred to (in which the personages involved, far from being innocent babes, are even supernaturally and ominously mature). In one perspective, the whole poem represents an effort to mediate by means of half-light, light as it were produced by darkness, the antinomy between day and night, and so between joy and sor-

[81] *Ibid.*
[82] *Ibid.*, p. 101.
[83] *Ibid.*, p. 267.

sow, between innocence and ominous wisdom. The possibility of such mediation is based upon faith in the efficacy of the poetic experience of nature.

The prose fragment "The Wanderings of Cain" (1798) [84] may be thought of as Coleridge's version of "The Waste Land," to which man is condemned when he ceases to be capable of the poetic experience of nature. The action takes place in a moon-lit wilderness. Like *The Ancient Mariner,* which, as Coleridge explains, "was written instead" when this subject was abandoned,[85] "The Wanderings of Cain" is the story of transgression, punishment, and redemption. The nature of the transgression is clearly stated in what E. H. Coleridge identifies as "a rough draft of a continuation or alternative version . . . found among Coleridge's papers."[86] Cain is being punished "because he neglected to make a proper use of his senses, etc."[87] And so in punishment he wanders among surroundings which in Coleridge's usual symbolic terminology are most conducive to "Joy," in wind and moonlight, and yet he says "the spirit within me is withered, and burnt up with extreme agony."[88] "The Mighty One . . . pursueth my soul like the wind, like the sandblast he passeth through me."[89] "The Mighty One who is against me speaketh in the wind of the cedar grove."[90] Just as the sailors were guilty in part by association with the Mariner, Cain's son is subjected to the consequences of his father's guilt—the happy squirrels that feed in the fir-trees leap away from him when he tries to play with them. The only lines of verse surviving, an introductory stanza, are concerned with the boy, and they are reminiscent of the paradox

[84] *Ibid.,* pp. 285-92.
[85] *Ibid.,* p. 287.
[86] *Ibid.,* p. 285*n.*
[87] *Ibid.*
[88] *Ibid.,* p. 292.
[89] *Ibid.,* p. 288.
[90] *Ibid.,* p. 289.

pointed out in "The Nightingale" when it is dealing with
Hartley in the moonlight:

> Encinctured with a twine of leaves,
> That leafy twine his only dress!
> A lovely Boy was plucking fruits,
> By moonlight in a wilderness.
> The moon was bright, the air was free,
> And fruits and flowers together grew
> On many a shrub and many a tree:
> And all put on a gentle hue,
> Hanging in the shadowy air
> Like a picture rich and rare.
> It was a climate where, they say,
> The night is more belov'd than day.
> But who that beauteous Boy beguil'd,
> That beauteous Boy to linger here?
> Alone, by night, a little child,
> In place so silent and so wild—
> Has he no friend, no loving mother near? [91]

In their wanderings, Cain and his son encounter the ghost of
Abel, who is bemoaning his fate, and the son says,

Ere yet I could speak, I am sure, O my father, that I heard that voice.
Have I not often said that I remembered a sweet voice? O my father!
this is it.[92]

Thus it is the child, able at least to look upon the squirrels with
love, as the Mariner looked upon the creatures of the sea, who
identifies the sweet voice out of the past,[93] and so leads to their
redemption, foreshadowed in the final passage of the fragment.
Cain has appealed to Abel to rescue him from his state of separation, and Abel answers,

[91] *Ibid.*, p. 287.
[92] *Ibid.*, p. 290.
[93] Cf. the song of the damsel with the dulcimer in "Kubla Khan."

O that thou hadst had pity on me as I will have pity on thee. Follow me, Son of Adam! and bring thy child with thee.

And they passed over the white sands between the rocks, silent as shadows.[94]

A poem based on a story as rich in symbolic possibilities as that of Cain and Abel is surely susceptible of interpretation on various levels, but one of the relevant ways of reading this fragment is to interpret it as an allegory of poetic catastrophe. This would be suggested immediately by what we know of the characteristic significance of moonlight in Coleridge's poetry, but the suggestion is reinforced by the echoes of other poems that we have just noted, and, most explicitly, by the statement concerning the misuse of the senses.[95] In 1798, Coleridge was not yet ready to write the poem in the first person, as he was to do in 1802 with "Dejection"; but he was already profoundly aware that the poetic experience could lead to the brink of strange and frightening abysses.

The use of starlight as a symbol of terror in "The Ballad of the Dark Ladie" (1798)[96] has already been pointed out.[97] The poem is primarily a love poem, and the symbolic force of the Ladie's terrified protest against her lover's suggestion that they "steal beneath the twinkling stars"[98] is difficult to decide upon with any certainty on the basis of anything suggested in what survives of the poem. But if we suppose that the starlight is here, as in so many other places, a symbol of the life of the imagination, of the poetic experience in all of its even sinister complexity, as Coleridge was beginning to know it, then the Ladie's terror seems appropriate. She has been thinking of their union in terms

[94] *Poems*, p. 292.
[95] See Warren, "A Poem of Pure Imagination," pp. 99 ff.
[96] *Poems*, pp. 293-95.
[97] See in this book pp. 42-44.
[98] *Poems*, p. 294.

of flower-girls and dancing, a wedding "in the eye of noon," leading to a natural human relationship; and she recoils from entering the mysterious, supernatural world into which her lover invites her.

The "Lines Written in the Album at Elbingrode, in the Hartz Forest" (1799) [99] contain the first explicit presage of "Dejection." As in "Dejection," Coleridge begins by describing the scene and the weather. Coming down the mountain, he is passing through fir groves "Where bright green moss heaves in sepulchral forms / Speckled with sunshine."

> And the breeze, murmuring indivisibly,
> Preserved its solemn murmur most distinct
> From many a note of many a waterfall,
> And the brook's chatter.[100]

Here are the elements associated throughout Coleridge's poetry, as we have seen, with the poetic experience of nature, the half-light, the breeze, and the mountain. He might be describing the very dell in which he imagines his friends to be wandering in "This Lime-Tree Bower,"[101] which was "only speckled by the midday sun," and whose imagined atmosphere had called forth the recollection:

> So my friend
> Struck with deep joy may stand, as I have stood,
> Silent with swimming sense; yea gazing round
> On the wide landscape, gaze till all doth seem
> Less gross than bodily; and of such hues
> As veil the Almighty Spirit, when yet he makes
> Spirits perceive his presence.[102]

[99] *Ibid.*, pp. 315-16.
[100] *Ibid.*, p. 315.
[101] See in this book pp. 95-96.
[102] *Poems*, p. 180.

At that time, in 1797, he had assured himself that

> Henceforth I shall know
> That Nature ne'er deserts the wise and pure;
> No plot so narrow, be but Nature there,
> No waste so vacant, but may well employ
> Each faculty of sense, and keep the heart
> Awake to Love and Beauty!

But now, having described the perfection of the scene before him, he says:

> I moved on
> In low and languid mood, for I had found
> That outward forms, the loftiest, still receive
> Their finest influence from the Life within;—
> Fair cyphers else: fair, but of import vague
> Or unconcerning, where the heart not finds
> History or prophecy of friend, or child,
> Or gentle maid, our first and early love,
> Or father, or the venerable name
> Of our adoréd country![103]

The low and languid mood is very close to the "wan and heart-less mood" of "Dejection"; and his explanation of it—

> That outward forms, the loftiest, still receive
> Their finest influence from the Life within;—

employs the very terms later to be used in "Dejection":

> I may not hope from outward forms to win
> The passion and the life, whose fountains are within.

Thus only fourteen months after the completion of *The Ancient Mariner,* only a year after he had enthusiastically reaffirmed the positive power of the "influxes" of nature in "The Nightingale," Coleridge found himself cut off from the poetic experience. Nature in itself was nothing but a cipher, that touches us only in

[103] *Ibid.,* pp. 315-16.

virtue of personal associations (which here constitute the "Life within"). When these lines were written, Coleridge had been in Germany for eight months, and he was terribly homesick. He thinks of England and the sight of sovran Brocken becomes feeble and dim. Yet it is clear that he is recording not just a passing mood of depression but a critical change in his inner life. The poem ends with these lines:

> Stranger, these impulses
> Blame thou not lightly; nor will I profane,
> With hasty judgment or injurious doubt,
> That man's sublimer spirit; who can feel
> That God is everywhere! the God who framed
> Mankind to be one mighty family,
> Himself our Father, and the World our Home.[104]

"That man's sublimer spirit" had been Coleridge's own spirit only recently, and he had obviously not reconciled himself to the loss of it. The full implications of its loss were not to be explored until three years later in "Dejection."

During these intervening three years, which witnessed one of the crucial events of Coleridge's life, his meeting and falling in love with Sara Hutchinson, his poetic production was very sparse in quantity and not very high in quality, unless, as Miss Schneider argues, "Kubla Khan" belongs in this period.[105] There is a large proportion of translations and imitations of German poems. His use of the symbols we are tracing indicates a continuing preoccupation with the nature of the poetic experience and the conditions of its occurrence, but the attitude expressed is remote and nostalgic. He is frequently writing about *other* people's poetic experiences and poems.[106]

[104] *Ibid.*, p. 316.

[105] *Coleridge, Opium, and "Kubla Khan,"* Chap. IV.

[106] See "Lines Composed in a Concert-Room," *Poems*, pp. 324-25; "Ode to Georgiana," *ibid.*, pp. 335-38; "A Stranger Minstrel," *ibid.*, pp. 350-52; "The Snow-Drop," *ibid.*, pp. 356-58.

In two short poems written in 1800, however, he is clearly dealing with experiences of his own. One of them, a poem of only eight lines, has the resounding title "Apologia Pro Sua Vita":

> The poet in his lone yet genial hour
> Gives to his eyes a magnifying power:
> Or rather he emancipates his eyes
> From the black shapeless accidents of size—
> In unctuous cones of kindling coal,
> Or smoke upwreathing from the pipe's trim bole,
>   His gifted eye can see
>   Phantoms of sublimity.[107]

The thought is ordinary enough, that by virtue of a special gift the poet sees correspondences that escape the common ken. But in the last line, in the choice of the word "phantom," there is a suggestion of irony. It is a long way, in any case, from "such hues / As veil the Almighty Spirit, when yet he makes / Spirits perceive his presence";[108] and still further from the "God / Diffused through all, that doth make all one whole."[109]

The other short poem is "A Thought Suggested by a View of Saddleback in Cumberland":

> On stern Blencartha's perilous height
>   The winds are tyrannous and strong;
> And flashing forth unsteady light
> From stern Blencartha's skiey height,
>   As loud the torrents throng!
> Beneath the moon, in gentle weather,
> They bind the earth and sky together.
> But oh! the sky and all its forms, how quiet!
> The things that seek the earth, how full of noise and riot![110]

[107] *Poems*, p. 345.
[108] *Ibid.*, p. 180.
[109] *Ibid.*, p. 114.
[110] *Ibid.*, p. 347.

The first seven of these lines might be the beginning of one of Coleridge's paeans to religious communication with nature— there is the wind, the moon, the mountain, and the rich image of the waterfalls binding earth and sky together under the influence of the moon. But the final couplet breaks the connection, and there is no more to be said.

Finally, a few months before "Dejection," there is the "Ode to Tranquillity" (1801).[111] Perhaps at no period in his life was Coleridge less qualified to write such an ode. But it is a kind of tranquillity of indifference he is seeking, and to which he is willing to dedicate the whole of his "feeling heart," his "searching soul":

> But me thy gentle hand will lead
> At morning through the accustomed mead;
> And in the sultry summer's heat
> Will build me up a mossy seat;
> And when the gust of Autumn crowds,
> And breaks the busy moonlight clouds,
> Thou best the thought canst raise, the heart attune,
> Light as the busy clouds, calm as the gliding moon.
>
> The feeling heart, the searching soul,
> To thee I dedicate the whole!
> And while within myself I trace
> The greatness of some future race,
> Aloof with hermit-eye I scan
> The present works of present man—
> A wild and dream-like trade of blood and guile,
> Too foolish for a tear, too wicked for a smile![112]

Two stanzas of the original version published in the *Morning Post* and later omitted make it clear that the context of the poem is political[113]—the trade of blood and guile is that of Napoleon;

111 *Ibid.*, pp. 360-61.
112 *Ibid.*, p. 361.
113 *Ibid.*, p. 360*n*.

but the "gust of Autumn" and the "moonlight clouds" suggest another level of meaning, a desire to move with tranquillity in the moon-world of the imagination, which Coleridge had stormed with such passionate ambition. But he was never to achieve the aloofness of the hermit-eye.

It may be helpful to list some of the things associated with the images we have traced; but caution is necessary. In the interest of discursive clarification, one may be tempted to go to the extreme of formulating a kind of schema, to say, for instance, that the half-lights "stand for" this, this, and this, the wind for this, this, and this, that the following are the relations among the symbols in each of these sets and between the two sets, and that it all adds up to—this. But the fact is that each of these images is inextricably imbedded in the unique context of the particular poem in which it occurs. The correspondences between the images and what they "stand for," and between the two families of images, the light images and wind images, are what we might call osmotic in character. Coleridge uses the word "translucence" in describing the relation between the thing symbolized and the symbol.[114] Although he was willing to speak of beauty as "the shorthand hieroglyphic of Truth," he was careful to point out that the knowledge achieved in the experience of beauty is "implicit knowledge—a silent communion of the Spirit with the Spirit in Nature, not without consciousness, though with the consciousness not successively unfolded."[115] Although each point in the schema, each definite, fixed associative equation, might have a real basis in the poem from which it was taken, isolation from its context automatically falsifies it to some degree. Meditating on this, one might be led to the opposite extreme, where one

---

[114] *The Statesman's Manual,* in *Works,* I, 437.
[115] Quoted by Muirhead, *Coleridge as Philosopher,* p. 195, from the Semina Rerum ms.

denies the possibility of any interpretation and takes the position that poems must only be "experienced," that any discursive analysis is not simply false but irrelevant.

Between these two extremes, that which would translate the poem into an abstract schema and that which would insist upon the pure experience of the poem, avoiding any analysis, there is the alternative of recognizing that it is not only possible but necessary to make analytical interpretations of poetic symbols, to talk about what symbols "mean," but that the purpose of doing so is not to take these meanings away as the "meaning" of the poem, but to return with them *to* the poem in order to re-experience it in the light of them. One moves from the direct experience, through a stage of "successive unfolding"—a stage with which few poems and perhaps no readers can dispense, back to an enriched experience. Actually, it is to be noted that the isolable "meaning" of many, perhaps most poems, even very great ones, is either trivial or obvious or both. We value them not for the information we get from them, the new or important things we may learn from them, but because there is a kind of miracle in the fact that even the tiniest scrap of meaning, of what we apprehend discursively with our intellects, can be incarnated in an object which we can feel, which we can experience immediately. In other words, it is not so much for new knowledge but for a new way of knowing what we may know best that we go to poems. It is surely something like this that Coleridge had in mind when he said that beauty is "the mediator between Truth and Feeling, the Head and the Heart," and when he defined imagination as

that reconciling and mediatory power, which incorporating the reason in images of the sense, and organizing (as it were) the flux of the sense by the permanence and self-circling energies of the reason, gives birth to a system of symbols, harmonious in themselves, and consubstantial with the truths of which they are conductors.[116]

What, then, in preparation for our examination of "Dejection," are some of the meanings incorporated in the sensory images of the half-lights and the wind in the poems we have gone through? Moonlight, starlight, twilight, and the other half-lights are most often, though not always, to be seen as furnishing the atmosphere in which certain experiences are environed, rather than as the active source of these experiences. They are, in different poems, the lights associated with, appropriate to, such things as:

Memory
Imagination
Absorption into Spirit
Dreams
Communion
Preternatural passions
Fancy
Visions
Inspiration
Mystical experiences.

The first thing to be noted is that all of these represent in some sense ways of knowing, and that they have in common the characteristic of being non-discursive, of being ways of knowing through immediate contact. *What* is known, literally speaking, is most frequently some insignificant particular, the scents snatched from a beanfield, the shadow of a leaf. It is the experience itself, the kind of immediate contact, that is emphasized. If I have what strikes me as a preternaturally intimate contact with something, so that the thing becomes somehow sacred to me, I may, in try-

[116] *The Statesman's Manual,* in *Complete Works,* I, 436.

ing to memorialize the event, in trying to capture and embody it, devote my major attention to the object to be created, to the task of taking from it and adding to it just those things that will make it capable of re-engendering the event; or, on the other hand, if I tend to introspection and great reflective awareness, I may dwell directly on the *experience* as such, devoting more care to describing *it* than to creating my object. Coleridge would seem to be doing the former in such lines as these from "The Eolian Harp":

> And now its strings
> Boldlier swept, the long sequacious notes
> Over delicious surges sink and rise,
> Such a soft floating witchery of sound
> As twilight Elfins make, when they at eve
> Voyage on gentle gales from Fairy-land,
> Where melodies round honey-dropping flowers,
> Footless and wild, like birds of Paradise,
> Nor pause, nor perch, hovering on untam'd wing![117]

The latter, and more frequent, tendency is exemplified in the following lines, addressed to the nightingale:

> But I *do* hear thee, and the high bough mark,
> Within whose mild moon-mellow'd foliage hid
> Thou warblest sad thy pity-pleading strains.
> O! I have listen'd, till my working soul,
> Waked by those strains to thousand phantasies,
> Absorb'd hath ceased to listen![118]

And this latter tendency is the stronger in proportion to the order of significance one consciously attaches to such experiences. For trivial as their immediate content may seem, their very occurrence may come to be taken as an indication of a fundamental and even supernatural truth. There is, for instance, the passage from "The Eolian Harp":

[117] *Poems*, p. 101.
[118] *Ibid.*, p. 93.

O! the one Life within us and abroad,
Which meets all motion and becomes its soul,
A light in sound, a sound-like power in light,
Rhythm in all thought, and joyance everywhere—
Methinks it should have been impossible
Not to love all things in a world so fill'd;
Where the breeze warbles, and the mute still air
Is Music slumbering on her instrument.[119]

Seven years later, after "Dejection," Coleridge wrote to Sotheby:

Never to see or describe any interesting appearance in nature without connecting it, by dim analogies, with the moral world proves faintness of impression. Nature has her proper interest, and he will know what it is who believes and feels that everything has a life of its own, and that we are all *One Life*. A poet's heart and intellect should be *combined,* intimately combined and unified with the great appearances of nature, and not merely held in solution and loose mixture with them in the shape of formal similes.[120]

The passage serves at the same time to reveal to us the order of significance that Coleridge attached to the poetic experience, and his critical awareness of one artistic danger of taking off from its immediacy into abstract speculation. As "Dejection" and his subsequent poetic career witness, he never fully grasped the moral and spiritual dangers of this inordinate reflexive concentration on and expectation of the poetic experience, although he felt their effects most drastically.

The atmosphere created by the half-lights is sometimes an atmosphere of joy, sometimes one of grief, sometimes a strange mixture of both. This fact furnishes as good an example as any of what Coleridge means when he says that a symbol, unlike allegory, "partakes of the reality which it renders intelligible."[121] The experience whose nature Coleridge is trying to communicate

119 *Ibid.,* p. 101. See in this book pp. 87-88.
120 *Letters,* I, 403-04.
121 *Statesman's Manual,* p. 437.

in these poems is distinguished by its very evanescence. It comes
like an unexpected and undeserved gift, and when it is fully
achieved the sense of fulfillment is almost overwhelming, analogous on the one hand to the experience of love, on the other hand
to the fulfillment of supernatural mystical contact, a loss of one's
separated identity to refind oneself with the object experienced—
an experience of what Coleridge calls "the One Life," which produces Joy. But it is *not* a direct contact with God, which would
involve and fulfill the whole being and in which one could rest.
Precisely in proportion to the depth of the soul it does reach, it
may seem to promise, to be about to be, something essentially
different and infinitely greater than it is, something of which it
is only a remote analogue. And so it is that the grief, the haunting
nostalgia, is instinct in the experience itself, along with the Joy,
as darkness is instinct in the "clouds, that late were rich with
light, Slow saddening round. . . ."[122] It is the kind of nostalgia
we sense in the most delicately joyous melody of Mozart. Baudelaire expresses the idea in these terms:

It is that immortal instinct for the beautiful which causes us to consider the earth and its spectacles as a glimpse, as a *correspondence* of
heaven. The insatiable thirst for all that is beyond what life reveals
is the most living proof of our immortality. It is at the same time by
means of poetry and by going beyond poetry, by means of and beyond music, that the soul glimpses the splendors that lie beyond the
tomb; and when an exquisite poem brings tears to the eyes, those
tears are not the proof of an excess of pleasure, they are much rather
the witnesses of an irritated melancholy, of an exasperated demand
of the nerves, of a nature exiled in the imperfect and wishing to seize
immediately, on this very earth, a revealed paradise.[123]

This passage can serve to illuminate a great many of the poems
we have been examining. It is through the ubiquitous half-light

122 *Poems,* p. 100.
123 Quoted by Jacques Maritain, *Situation of Poetry,* p. 43.

images that Coleridge communicates a similar apprehension. In "Kubla Khan" we have perhaps the most perfect evocation of Baudelaire's "revealed paradise."

While, as we have seen, the half-lights are most often seen as furnishing the atmosphere in which the poetic experience occurs, the passively favorable environment as it were, the wind serves most often as an exciting agent. It is spoken of as

> the voice of spirit
> the destroyer of spiritual power
> the destroyer of visions
> the destroyer of dreams
> the stimulant of the imagination
> the source of ecstasy
> the source of creative agitation
> the Holy Spirit
> an evil tumult
> solemn music
> the theme of poetry
> a divine voice.

Just as the half-lights betoken joy and grief, so the wind is both inspirer and destroyer. In fact, as close examination of the poems reveals, the symbolic equivalents are not so neatly distinguished as the lists given might suggest: the half-lights are sometimes envisaged as active inspiring agents, the wind sometimes envisaged as furnishing the conducive atmosphere. Sometimes the fusion of images is complete:

> A light in sound, a sound-like power in light,
> Rhythm in all thought, and joyance everywhere.

In the actual throes of poetic communion, the distinctions are blurred to the point of irrelevance. But from time immemorial

the wind has seemed to furnish an apt symbol for active inspiration. It is subtle and pervasive. At the same time, there is the
fact that it "bloweth where it listeth." And it is by turns a source
of refreshment and invigoration or of ruthless destruction. The
same wind, with the same force, may destroy or not, depending
upon the amount of surface an object exposes to it and the sure-
ness of the object's foundations.

IV

"DEJECTION"

When one turns from the perusal of all these poems, written over a period of fourteen years, between the ages of sixteen and thirty, all of them dealing with or alluding to the poetic experience, when one turns from these poems to "Dejection," it is immediately evident that from the motto all the way through the poem Coleridge is dealing with symbols that constitute the very weather of his mind, symbols whose changes of significance for him constitute a kind of history of his spiritual development.

He was reminded of the stanza from "Sir Patrick Spence" quite simply, perhaps, by the phase of the moon on the night when he composed "Dejection";[1] but the correspondences of this stanza with the mood expressed in the poem are remarkably complex and warrant some attention. In the version Coleridge prefixed to his poem, the stanza embraces two of his favorite symbols, and by means of a bit of folk meteorology welds them together:

> Late, late yestreen I saw the new Moon,
> With the old Moon in her arms;
> And I fear, I fear, my Master dear!
> We shall have a deadly storm.

[1] Although it is possible, as Lowes suggests (*Road to Xanadu,* p. 174), that he borrowed the image from Dorothy Wordsworth.

But it would appear that in order to achieve this effect Coleridge doctored the ballad as he found it in Percy's *Reliques*. In Percy the moon and the storm appear in two succeeding stanzas:

> 'Mak hast, mak haste, my mirry men all,
> Our guid schip sails the morne;'
> 'O say na sae, my master deir,
> For I feir a deadlie storme.
>
> 'Late, late yestreen I saw the new moon,
> Wi' the auld moone in her arme;
> And I feir, I feir, my deir master,
> That we will com to harme.'[2]

It is perhaps more likely that Coleridge made the transposition unconsciously in recalling the ballad from memory than that he made it deliberately, with the Percy version in front of him; but the alteration is none the less significant in the indication it gives of the importance he attached to the juxtaposition of the two images. There is little doubt that Coleridge was using Percy's version, since no other known version available at the time corresponds at all closely to the stanza as Coleridge presents it,[3] with modernized spelling and one or two other minor variations.

The state of mind Coleridge is trying to realize artistically in "Dejection" is one of paradox and contradiction. In the ballad stanza the moon, the new moon, ordinarily associated with things tender, delicate, and young, is the harbinger of a "deadly storm," because it is not just the new moon at all, but the moon in its most ambiguous state, "the new Moon, / With the old Moon in her arms," an intimate juxtaposition of the young and promising with the wasted and worn-out. It is this juxtaposition that was wreaking destruction in Coleridge's inner life, and that forms the subject matter of "Dejection."

[2] See Francis J. Child, *English and Scottish Ballads* (Boston: Little, Brown, 1860), III, 150.
[3] *Ibid.*, pp. 147-56, 338-42.

In his own description of the moon in the poem, he adds details of lighting which are just those associated in the past with his most exalted moments of communion with Nature:

> For lo! the New-moon winter-bright!
> And overspread with phantom light,
> (With swimming phantom light o'erspread
> But rimmed and circled by a silver thread)
> I see the old Moon in her lap, foretelling
> The coming on of rain and squally blast.[4]

This is, if one likes, very accurate, if heightened, "nature description." But it is also highly functional imagery, reinforcing the peculiar symbolic significance of the moon in the poem. Always somehow ambivalent, unstable (and therefore more precious[5]), the moon is here presented in its most ambivalent phase, and this fact is emphasized by the details that Coleridge adds to the description in the ballad, to symbolize the fragile, elusive character of the origin of the poetic experience, of the state in which it occurs.

The ambivalence is compounded by the fact that the moon presages a storm, but a *wished-for* storm:

> And oh! that even now the gust were swelling,
> And the slant night-shower driving loud and fast!
> Those sounds which oft have raised me, whilst they awed,
> And sent my soul abroad,
> Might now perhaps their wonted impulse give,
> Might startle this dull pain, and make it move and live![6]

The wind itself is ambivalent as a conventional symbol, as is Coleridge's use of it. Its traditional significance goes at least back to the book of Genesis, in which it is said that "the Lord God

[4] *Poems,* p. 363.
[5] See "Absence," discussed in this book pp. 70-71.
[6] *Poems,* p. 363.

formed man of the dust of the ground, and breathed into his nostrils the breath of life, and man became a living soul."[7] It is the age-old symbol of inspiration, of the divine afflatus. But becoming a storm, a tempest, it brings with it destruction and disaster. Yet Coleridge wishes for a storm, a real storm with swelling gust and "slant night-shower driving loud and fast," hoping to be uplifted and exhilarated by it. Praying for the wind of inspiration is always dangerous, although the stronger the wind one can withstand this side of annihilation the greater the result; and the ballad predicts a "deadly storm." That is what arrives in Stanza VII of "Dejection." But it is deadly in two almost contradictory senses. It is deadly in the sense of being a killer—it speaks to Coleridge of a "host in rout, / With groans, of trampled men, with smarting wounds"; and at the same time it is deadly in the negative sense—it fails to quicken, to make Coleridge's dull pain move and live. Far from arousing his poetic powers, as he had vaguely hoped, the storm cannot even kill them, because they are already dead. In this light, the fate of Sir Patrick and his men is to be preferred.

Coleridge adds another dimension to the paradox by describing the moon as "winter-bright." He is writing in the month of April, as we discover without the aid of external evidence from his address to the storm when it comes:

> Mad Lutanist! who in this month of showers,
> Of dark-brown gardens, and of peeping flowers,
> Mak'st Devils' yule, with worse than wintry song,
> The blossoms, buds, and timorous leaves among.[8]

A cold, aloof winter moon in April—we are reminded at once of the "inanimate cold world" contrasted with the "fair luminous cloud" in Stanza IV. Coleridge is likely to have had in his mind

[7] II:7.
[8] *Poems*, p. 367.

or under his eye, not just the lines he used as a motto, but the whole of "Sir Patrick Spence." The stanza just preceding the lines he used introduces this note of unseasonableness:

> O what is this has done this deid,
>   This ill deid don to me,
> To send me out this time o' yeir,
>   To sail upon the se![9]

Like Sir Patrick, Coleridge's soul has been "sent abroad," only to find itself now "upon a lonesome wild" (line 121). Sir Patrick was sent out at the wrong time of year, whereas Coleridge finds himself at the right time of year for the kind of voyage he projects, yet unable to weigh anchor. In his earlier, uneasily pantheistic days, he had written the lines:

> There is one Mind, one omnipresent Mind,
> Omnific. His most holy name is Love.
> Truth of subliming import! with the which
> Who feeds and saturates his constant soul,
> He from his small particular orbit flies
> With blest outstarting! From himself he flies,
> Stands in the sun, and with no partial gaze
> Views all creation; and he loves it all,
> And blesses it, and calls it very good!
> This is indeed to dwell with the Most High!
> Cherubs and rapture-trembling Seraphim
> Can press no nearer to the Almighty's throne.[10]

It is of such moments of "blest outstarting" that Coleridge is thinking, when he speaks of

> Those sounds which oft have raised me, whilst they awed,
>   And sent my soul abroad.

[9] Child, *English and Scottish Ballads*, p. 150.
[10] *Poems*, p. 113, "Religious Musings."

If at the end of the poetic voyage, if from the poetic contact with nature, he expected, as the passage from "Religious Musings" clearly implies, to find the beatific vision, union with God in love, then it is not surprising that not finding it he lacked the heart to re-embark, at least after a certain number of voyages which in this perspective ended in failure.

The whole story of Sir Patrick Spence, being the account of a voyage ending in disaster, must have appealed to Coleridge as a partial prototype of *The Ancient Mariner*. Unlike the Mariner, however, Sir Patrick went down with his crew, and for that reason the ballad furnishes a more appropriate motto for "Dejection" than would a stanza from *The Ancient Mariner,* for there is no suggestion of rescue or salvation for the reluctant mariner in "Dejection." The Ancient Mariner's salvation is achieved by virtue of just such a "blest outstarting" as Coleridge had described in "Religious Musings." In "The Nightingale" (1798), he was still sure that if one only left oneself open to nature's influxes instead of giving oneself up to artificialities, one would "share in Nature's immortality."[11] And he said that he and Wordsworth and Dorothy had learned to do just that. In "Dejection," it is the very instrument of salvation which has failed him, or rather is no longer available to him. There would seem to be an element of undeserved and irrevocable punishment in "Dejection" as in "Sir Patrick Spence." Coleridge seems to himself to have *done* that which he ought to have done, and still there is no health in him.

These are some of the symbolic relations that seem to exist between the "grand old Ballad" and Coleridge's poem, and, as we have seen, they carry us into the heart of the poem. Other correspondences of a subtler kind can be suggested. The tender image of the new moon with the old moon "in her arms," fol-

[11] *Ibid.,* p. 265.

lowed by "I fear, I fear," this juxtaposition of love and fear,[12] might remind us that in its original version Coleridge's poem was a love letter written to Sara Hutchinson. That version contains 340 lines, as compared with 139 lines in the published versions. Many of the additional lines are expressions of melancholy affection, in which Coleridge conceives of all the pleasure he might have had in being with his love as "a dim Dream of Pain to follow!" And we remember the ladies "wi their gold kems in their hair, / Waiting for their ain deir lords."

Taken out of their immediate context, the very first words of the ballad stanza set the tone for the whole of Coleridge's poem: "Late, late. . . ." It is indeed late for Coleridge at this point. "Dejection" is an "afterwards" poem. It begins on a casual, nostalgic, musing note:

> Well! If the Bard was weather-wise, who made
>   The grand old ballad of Sir Patrick Spence,
>   This night, so tranquil now, will not go hence
> Unroused by winds, that ply a busier trade
> Than those which mould yon cloud in lazy flakes,
> Or the dull sobbing draft, that moans and rakes
> Upon the strings of this Æolian lute,
>   Which better far were mute.[13]

Beginning with "Well!", the tone is that of someone being, or trying to be, remote and philosophical about a struggle that is over, and lost. The reference to the ballad is a little playful, affectionately patronizing: it's a grand old ballad, but perhaps not to be taken too seriously in meteorological terms. Nevertheless, we'll play along with the idea. Even Coleridge's beloved double negative serves its purpose here in creating an atmosphere of detachment:

[12] See in this book pp. 47 ff.
[13] *Poems,* pp. 362-63.

>   This night, so tranquil now, will not go hence
>   Unroused by winds, that ply a busier trade.

The ironic understatement of "ply a busier trade," achieved
through the inappropriateness of the commercial metaphor, contributes still further to this mood of indifference. The cloud is
being moulded in "lazy" flakes—not an especially likely adjective
to describe cloud-flakes. And the Æolian lute, which seven years.
before had merited a whole enthusiastic poem, is dismissed in one
short, terse line.

After all this, the beginning of the second sentence of the poem
comes as a surprise: "For lo! the New-moon winter-bright!" And
the remaining lines of the stanza rise to a full crescendo, describing the remembered storm of the poetic experience, only to
fall again, with the final couplet, into nostalgia:

>   Those sounds . . .
>   Might now perhaps their wonted impulse give,
>   Might startle this dull pain, and make it move and live!

This first stanza is thus a miniature of the poem as a whole.

The last line of the first stanza deserves special attention. It is
one of the fine strokes of which there are so many in Coleridge's
poems—found often even in his second-rate poems. Some of these
passages are brilliant examples of his sensitivity in observing and
imaginatively recording nature:

>   When mountain surges bellowing deep
>   With an uncouth monster-leap
>   Plung'd foaming on the shore.[14]

Sometimes they are instances of what can only be called Coleridgean magic, a kind of extravagant imaginative flight in which
the willing suspension of disbelief is induced by the sober serious-

---

[14] *Ibid.,* p. 98.

ness of the poet, as reflected in the careful accuracy of his language and imagery:

> Such a soft floating witchery of sound
> As twilight Elfins make, when they at eve
> Voyage on gentle gales from Fairy-land,
> Where Melodies round honey-dropping flowers,
> Footless and wild, like birds of Paradise,
> Nor pause, nor perch, hovering on untam'd wing![15]

And sometimes they grow out of his uncanny accuracy in the observation and expression of psychological states—a pain that "moves and lives!" But they are none of them scattered gems. Their effectiveness derives not only from the sources mentioned but from their place in the structure of the poems in which they occur. This last line of the first stanza of "Dejection" is crucial to the interpretation of the poem and to its biographical significance. In July, 1802, four months after the composition of "Dejection," he wrote to Southey that he attributed his loss of poetic genius

to my long and exceedingly severe metaphysical investigations, and these partly to private afflictions which rendered any subjects immediately concerned with feeling, a source of pain and disquiet to me.[16]

In the *Biographia Literaria* he speaks of having "sought a refuge from bodily pain and mismanaged sensibility in abstruse researches, which exercised the strength and subtlety of the understanding without awakening the feelings of the heart."[17] In both of these instances, and in others, he seems to be saying that in avoiding poetry he was trying to *avoid* having his feelings awakened. Here, on the contrary, he is complaining of an *absence* of feeling, imploring that it be awakened, even in the form of pain. Stanza II describes his present state in detail:

[15] *Ibid.*, p. 101.
[16] *Letters*, I, 388 (quoted in this book p. 14).
[17] I, 10.

A grief without a pang, void, dark, and drear,
A stifled, drowsy, unimpassioned grief,
Which finds no natural outlet, no relief,
 In word, or sigh, or tear—
O Lady! in this wan and heartless mood,
To other thoughts by yonder throstle woo'd,
 All this long eve, so balmy and serene,
Have I been gazing on the western sky,
 And its peculiar tint of yellow green:
And still I gaze—and with how blank an eye!
And those thin clouds above, in flakes and bars,
That give away their motion to the stars;
Those stars, that glide behind them or between,
Now sparkling, now bedimmed, but always seen:
Yon crescent Moon, as fixed as if it grew
In its own cloudless, starless lake of blue;
I see them all so excellently fair,
I see, not feel, how beautiful they are![18]

Again, as in his description of the moon in Stanza I, this passage reveals very close *observation of nature,* but the details Coleridge notes are, in addition, a function of the theme of the poem. The clouds *"give away* their motion to the stars"; the moon is "In its own cloudless, starless lake of blue." There is still a natural communion and kinship among the things of nature. The stars, though sometimes sparkling and sometimes bedimmed, are *"always seen";* the moon is *"fixed* as if it *grew* / In its own cloudless, starless lake of blue." There is still in nature stability in motion, something abiding through change. For Coleridge communion has ceased, and there is no stability.

In Stanza III he goes on:

> My genial spirits fail;
> And what can these avail
> To lift the smothering weight from off my breast?

[18] *Poems,* p. 364.

> It were a vain endeavor,
> Though I should gaze forever
> On that green light that lingers in the west.[19]

The implication is that any spontaneous movement of feeling, even a sharp pang of grief, would be welcome, and yet he is totally incapable of it, though we know how often in the past that green light in the west had aroused him. After two stanzas in which he describes what it is he has lost (Joy) and gives a philosophical explanation of its loss, he gives in Stanza VI the biographical account of what has happened:

> There was a time when, though my path was rough,
>   This joy within me dallied with distress,
> And all misfortunes were but as the stuff
>   Whence Fancy made me dreams of happiness:
> For hope grew round me, like the twining vine,
> And fruits and foliage, not my own, seemed mine.
> But now afflictions bow me down to earth:
> Nor care I that they rob me of my mirth;
>   But oh! each visitation
> Suspends what nature gave me at my birth,
>   My shaping spirit of Imagination.[20]

This would seem to constitute a clear denial that afflictions were the *cause* of the change. He had had afflictions before, serious afflictions, but far from killing "Joy," they furnished material for Fancy, they fostered poetry, because he still had "hope" (for ultimate fulfillment, mystical fulfillment, in love and in poetry). The word "dallied" is well-chosen: in love, impediments are a source of pleasure when we are sure of attaining the goal. It is just possible that there is an echo of Milton's "Let our frail thoughts dally with false surmise."[21] But now afflictions bow

[19] *Ibid.,* p. 365.
[20] *Ibid.,* p. 366.
[21] *Lycidas,* line 153.

him down to earth. There is no explanation here of *why* he had
lost hope, and therefore "Joy," but only the statement that he
has lost them, and that as a result afflictions, instead of being grist
for the mill of artistic creation, suspend its operation. The "shaping spirit of Imagination" can be understood to refer to the artistic elaboration of poetic experience, as distinguished from the
poetic experience itself (which is "Joy"). And once the poetic
experience, once "Joy" is gone, the source of artistic creation is
cut off.

In the letter version of "Dejection" twenty-two lines are inter-
posed here in the effort to make clear what is meant by "afflictions":

> I speak not now of those habitual ills
> That wear out Life, when two unequal Minds
> Meet in one House and two discordant Wills—
>   This leaves me, where it finds,
> Past cure, and past Complaint,—a fate austere
> Too fix'd and hopeless to partake of Fear!
> But thou, dear Sara (dear indeed thou art,
> My Comforter, a Heart within my Heart!)
> Thou, and the Few, we love, tho' few ye be,
> Make up a world of Hopes and Fears for me.
> And if affliction, or distemp'ring Pain,
> Or wayward Chance befall you, I complain
> Not that I mourn—O friends, most dear! most true!
>   Methinks to weep with you
> Were better far than to rejoice alone—
> But that the coarse domestic Life has shown
> No Habits of heart-nursing Sympathy,
> No Griefs but such as dull and deaden me,
> No mutual mild Enjoyments of it's own,
> No Hopes of its own Vintage, None O! none—
> Whence when I mourn'd for you, my Heart might borrow
> Fair forms and living Motions for its Sorrow.[22]

[22] Whalley, *Coleridge and Sara Hutchinson*, pp. 161-62, lines 243-64.

This is a curious statement. The afflictions that "bow him down to earth" are not his domestic difficulties, to which he is more or less stoically reconciled by now, so that he feels neither hope nor fear in connection with them. Rather, the possibility of a new world of hopes and fears has opened up before him—the world consisting of his relationships with the Wordsworths and with Sara Hutchinson (a complete world of poetry and love); and he is complaining not that it is the occasion of mourning and fear but that he is unable to respond to the occasions it offers (just as he is unable to respond to the incitements of nature). His explanation of why he cannot respond to them, of why he cannot feel the appropriate fears and sorrows, is the curious part of the statement: he cannot feel them because his domestic life has not offered the occasion for such fears and sorrows, and as a result he has not formed the habit of feeling such things. Now, when a real occasion does present itself, there is nowhere for his heart to "borrow / Fair forms and living Motions for its sorrow." The conception of psychological operations which seems to underlie this analysis is highly suspect. If Sara Hutchinson read this passage carefully, she might well have been unfavorably impressed by his feeling the necessity to borrow forms and motions from his previous relationship in order to react to her. Coleridge goes on, in lines which form the concluding part of Stanza VI in the published versions, to explain how this has come about in terms of his own maneuverings:

> For not to think of what I needs must feel,
>   But to be still and patient, all I can;
> And haply by abstruse research to steal
>   From my own nature all the natural man—
>   This was my sole resource, my only plan:
> Till that which suits a part infects the whole,
> And now is almost grown the habit of my soul.[23]

23 *Poems*, p. 367.

It is hard not to see some contradiction or at least confusion here. The whole interpretation hinges on what he means by saying that his sole resource is "not to think of what I needs must feel." The most obvious sense of those words would be that he was trying (by diverting himself into abstruse research) not to feel things he was forced by circumstances to feel, e.g., the cruel disappointments and vexations of his domestic life; and that what began as a defense mechanism against too acute feelings in a particular connection had become generalized as a habit affecting other departments of his life. But in the letter version quoted he has complained, precisely, that he cannot feel now, in response to genuine occasions for feeling, because his marriage was so *lacking* in such occasions that he has never developed the habit. In the light of this, it would seem that the line in question should be read: "In order to spare myself the pain of thinking about what I ought to be having in the way of feeling in connection with my marriage, I made the attempt to kill my capacity for such feelings by indulging in abstruse researches." We are thus faced with a choice of contradictions. If we read the line in the former way, it is in contradiction with its context in the poem. If we read it in the latter way, it is in contradiction with the clear intent of Coleridge's various prose statements concerning his flight from poetry into metaphysics because poetry aroused his feelings.

In any case, we are forced by all that we know of Coleridge's life prior to the moment of "Dejection," as well as by other things he says in the poem, to reject the account he presents in the passage quoted above from the letter version of the poem. It is simply not true, by Coleridge's own testimony,[24] that his "coarse domestic life" had known

---

[24] See in this book Chap. II.

> No Habits of heart-nursing Sympathy,
> No Griefs but such as dull and deaden me,
> No mutual mild Enjoyments of its own,
> No hopes of its own Vintage,

His domestic life had, in spite of everything, known a great deal of feeling—a great many mild enjoyments and keen griefs. He speaks of one of the latter in a passage immediately following, in connection with his children:

> My little children are a Joy, a Love,
>   A good Gift from above!
> But what is Bliss, that still calls up a Woe,
>   And makes it doubly keen
> Compelling me to *feel,* as well as *know*
> What a most blessed Lot mine might have been.[25]

The italics are Coleridge's. Here at least is one grief that was keen, not dull and deadening. In short, his picture of his marriage as an emotional blank is simply not true to fact; and even if it were, there is no plausible psychological reason why this fact should render him incapable of feeling when the occasion presented itself, given even the intervention of a great deal of abstruse research. Coleridge is obviously casting about desperately in his effort to understand what has happened to him, and he is perhaps overanxious to denude his marriage of significance in describing it to Sara Hutchinson. In addition, he is repeatedly telling Sara in this letter that he cannot feel what he ought to feel toward *her,* and one way of explaining this most disturbing and reprehensible fact is to blame it all on his marriage.

As we know by his own account, his life had been full of griefs, and yet for a considerable period this had not inhibited his capacity for emotional involvement (he was still able to fall deeply

[25] Lines 272-77 of the letter version, Whalley, *Coleridge and Sara Hutchinson,* p. 162.

in love with Sara Hutchinson in 1799). Nor, as he says in a passage quoted ("There was a time when, though my path was rough . . .") did his griefs inhibit his poetic experience. We have already examined the relation between his metaphysical research and his poetic activities, and found that his griefs were by no means at the origin of his metaphysical research, and that even if they did lead him to intensify it, the research cannot be assigned as the cause of his poetic atrophy, since the intensification antedated his best poetic work.

Finally, even if metaphysical research had been undertaken as an autotherapeutic measure either to deaden pain or to compensate for the absence of feeling, one must again question the psychological plausibility of Coleridge's explanation that "that which suits a part" (the intellectual attitude appropriate to metaphysical research, the abstractive attitude) "infects the whole." Such a cross-infection of the poetic by the abstractive function cannot seriously be thought to take place by a kind of simple contagion. For this to take place, the poetic function itself would have to be receptive to the disease by virtue of some intrinsic defect or weakness. But it seems that this whole physiological metaphor is inappropriate and misleading. Coleridge is speaking of metaphysics as if it were a kind of narcotic he took to deaden the pain in one part of his body, and which did so more or less successfully but in the process deadened his other members as well. The metaphor is psychologically unsound. The fact seems to be that though Coleridge's description of the symptoms is masterful, his whole presentation of the psychological case history of this most important development in his life is confused, contradictory, and factually inaccurate. This may seem a surprising thing to say about the subtle-souled psychologist. But is it so surprising after all? Quite simply, if he had understood what was happening to him and why, he would not be the Coleridge we know.

It is important to note here that Stanza VI, with which we have been dealing, the case-history stanza, is the only one in the poem which is completely out of reference with the symbolic structure of the poem. It is a poem about the poetic experience and the incapacity for it in which Coleridge found himself. In describing the resulting state in Stanzas I, II, III, VII, and VIII, and in his philosophical reflections in Stanzas IV and V, he employs in a highly organic way the symbols which were perennially associated in his mind with the poetic experience—light and wind. Only in Stanza VI are these symbols totally absent. In that respect it is like a parenthesis in the poem. There are many such parentheses in the longer letter version, but all except this one were omitted in the published versions. And this one was itself pruned of twenty-two lines.[26] Yet this is, in one perspective, the crucial stanza of the poem, the one that attempts to tell how he came to be in a state of dejection—why the rest of the poem ever came to be written.

We have still to consider what may be called the central section of the poem, its climax, the lines in which Coleridge reflects philosophically, not on the causes of his own loss of "Joy," but on what such a loss entails, and why. This section begins with the final couplet of Stanza III:

> I may not hope from outward forms to win
> The passion and the life, whose fountains are within.

> IV

> O Lady! we receive but what we give,
> And in our life alone does Nature live:
> Ours is her wedding garment, ours her shroud!
>   And would we aught behold, of higher worth,
> Than that inanimate cold world allowed
> To the poor loveless ever-anxious crowd,

[26] For Coleridge's own comment on the poetic quality of this stanza, see in this book p. 130.

> Ah! from the soul itself must issue forth
> A light, a glory, a fair luminous cloud
>   Enveloping the Earth—
> And from the soul itself there must be sent
>   A sweet and potent voice, of its own birth,
> Of all sweet sounds the life and element![27]

This passage may be read simply as an objective description of
the poetic relation between man and nature, an examination of
the part contributed by man and the part contributed by nature
to the experience which issues in a new creation, a new object
which is the work of art. In the final couplet of Stanza III, is
Coleridge simply uttering the truism that the poet must do his
part, must be alive to the life of nature, if the poetic experience
is to take place? It is easy to overlook the comma in line 46, which
makes of the clause "whose fountains are within" a nonrestrictive clause, and to read the line as implying that *some* of the passion and life come from within the poet. In this case the lines
would be a tautology, saying simply that one cannot find outside
what can only be found inside. But the comma is there, the clause
is nonrestrictive, and Coleridge obviously does not intend to state
a simple tautology. He is saying that the fountains of passion and
life are inside the poet and *only* there, and, by implication, that
nature furnishes only inanimate raw material. This is made
explicit in Stanza IV: "we receive but what we give, / And in
our life alone does Nature live." The world (in itself, as perceived
by the passive crowd) is an "inanimate cold world," comprising
in itself no "higher worth." In a passage in the letter version
which immediately follows "The passion and the life, whose
fountains are within," he refers even more disdainfully to "These
lifeless Shapes, around, below, / Above," and asks, "O what can
they impart?"[28] And the metaphors he uses concerning what

[27] *Poems,* p. 365, lines 45-58.
[28] Whalley, *Coleridge and Sara Hutchinson,* p. 156.

the poet contributes carry the idea still further—the poet puts a garment on nature, a wedding garment or a shroud; the fair luminous cloud that issues from the soul "envelops" the earth.

It is worth pausing to notice the succession of images in line 54. Coleridge says that from the soul must issue forth "A light, a glory, a fair luminous cloud." In one sense he seems to be struggling for just the right term (and not quite content with any of these three, he switches later to an auditory image); but there is, all the same, an order discernible in the series of images, an order of increasing impressiveness (a glory is more impressive than a mere light, a fair luminous cloud at least somehow vaster than a glory). At the same time there is an order of decreasing clarity of illumination. By the time we arrive at the fair luminous cloud, we have something that really tends to hide nature rather than to show it forth. This is a light not to see by but to keep from seeing clearly by—it is a covering, a garment. This is apparently the same diffused half-light that we have met throughout Coleridge's earlier poetry, but the difference here is twofold, and critical: up to this point, the poet has not been the source of it, and, though a half-light, it has been a light to see by, and to see a thoroughly animate nature.

One element in this and the following stanza may seem to present a difficulty in connection with this interpretation of the poem as a complete reversal of Coleridge's previous views concerning the highly animate and generative character of nature. Already in Stanza IV, one of the garments with which we may clothe nature is a "wedding garment." If nature is really cold and inanimate, only the shroud, not the wedding garment would seem appropriate—one does not ordinarily think of wedding a corpse. One is inclined to suppose that if nature can become our bride, there must be some life left in her.

It might be possible to assume that Coleridge threw in this contrast for immediate effect, without intending its implications to be carried through the rest of the passage. But in Stanza V we have the lines (67-71):

> Joy, Lady! is the spirit and the power,
> Which wedding Nature to us gives in dower
>   A new Earth and new Heaven
> Undreamt of by the sensual and the proud—
> Joy is the sweet voice, Joy the luminous cloud—[29]

The wedding metaphor is obviously an integral element of this whole section of the poem (Stanzas IV and V). Because of the absence of punctuation in line 68 ("Which wedding Nature to us gives in dower"), several significantly conflicting interpretations are grammatically possible, depending on what one takes to be the ultimate subject of the verb "gives." There are three possibilities: "Joy," "wedding," and "Nature."

If "Joy" is the subject, then "wedding" may be taken as a gerund, object of an understood preposition, and the lines are to be read as saying that Joy is the spirit and the power which, in wedding nature to us, gives us a new earth and heaven as a dowry. Richards reads the lines in this way, insinuating "in," and, whether by accident or intention, actually adding a comma after "us" in line 68. He speaks of

> the Joy which in
>
>   wedding Nature to us, gives in dower
>   A new Earth and new Heaven.[30]

But the lines may also be read in the following way (since in fact no preposition occurs before "wedding" and there are no commas to set off "wedding Nature to us" as a nonrestrictive phrase): "The fact of wedding ourselves to Nature gives us the

[29] *Poems,* p. 366.
[30] *Coleridge on Imagination,* p. 151.

spirit and power which are Joy, at the same time that it confers life upon the previously inanimate bride." In this reading "wedding" is a gerund, subject of "gives." Then "A new Earth and new Heaven" would be in some kind of apposition with "dower," an apposition implying something like "[thus producing] a new Earth and new Heaven." This reading, like that of Richards, would preserve what Richards calls the "projective" view[31] of the poetic experience which is reflected in the rest of the poem. But supposing this to be Coleridge's intention, the absence of a comma after "dower" would have to be taken as a simple but serious oversight on Coleridge's part. This is perhaps what H. N. Coleridge supposed when he inserted the comma after "dower" in the edition of 1834.[32] In addition to this, there is the difficulty that in this reading it is the *fact of our wedding* that presents the dowry, whereas properly it is the bride's father or perhaps the bride who customarily presents a dowry.

Finally, it would be possible to read "wedding" not as a gerund, either subject of "gives" or object of an understood preposition, but as a participial adjective modifying "Nature." In this case the lines would be saying that Joy is the spirit and the power which Nature gives us as a dowry on the occasion of our wedding with her. "A new Earth and new Heaven" would still, as in the previous reading, be left more or less dangling. Most important, this reading would be in direct contradiction with all Coleridge has said in the preceding lines, and in the lines which immediately follow. He would be saying that the spirit and the power (the passion and the life of Stanza III) are received *from* Nature.

Thus Richards' reading seems to be the most satisfactory, since

---

[31] *Ibid.,* pp. 145 ff.
[32] See H. W. Garrod, "Dejection: an Ode, lines 67-70. Punctuation," *Times Literary Supplement,* May 4, 1922, p. 292; May 11, 1922, p. 308.

the omissions it presupposes are of a fairly conventional kind,[33] and since it is consistent with the rest of the poem. But we are still left with a kind of inconsistency, or with a rather cumbersome and strained metaphor: Joy, a spirit which for all we can tell from the poem, has its origin wholly within us, assumes the figure of an independent being which acts as priest in performing the wedding between us and nature and also as father of the bride, since he gives the dowry (a new Earth and new Heaven), which, curiously enough, is the bride herself, previously dead, now brought to life—a fantastic ceremony, all in all. Paraphrased into more abstract terms, the lines would seem to be saying something like this: "Joy is that frame of mind which enables us to desire and consummate a personal union with an inanimate object and in doing so to cause the object to come alive." The prototype of the poet would be Pygmalion, though even Pygmalion had to pray to Aphrodite in order to bring Galatea to life. To come closer to Coleridge's habitual terminology, the poet's joy in creation would be compared to God's joy in creating man out of the dust of the earth—the poet would breathe the breath of life into nature in order that he might, as it were, receive its love in return (nature is, after all, the bride), and as a result know joy. In this state of joy he would produce works of art (a remarkable case of doing something greater in order to accomplish something lesser in the same order). Everything would be coming from the poet. He would be creating if not *ex nihilo,* then out of chaos.

Some sixty years earlier, Edward Young had given an apparently similar account of things in the fifth section of "Night Thoughts":

[33] Short parenthetical phrases are often not set off by commas, and the ellipsis involved in writing "wedding Nature to us" for "in wedding Nature to us" is not of an uncommon sort; whereas the omission of a comma between a substantive

Our senses, as our reason, are divine.
But for the magic organ's powerful charm,
Earth were a rude, uncolor'd chaos still.
Objects are but th' occasion; ours th' exploit;
Ours is the cloth, the pencil, and the paint,
Which nature's admirable picture draws
And beautifies creation's ample dome.
Like Milton's Eve, when gazing on the lake,
Man makes the matchless image, man admires:
Say then, shall man, his thoughts all sent abroad,
Superior wonders in himself forgot,
His admiration waste on objects round,
When heaven makes him the soul of all he sees [?] [34]

Reading it in one way this would seem to be an exaggeration of neoclassical doctrine, putting all the emphasis on artistic elaboration, on what art does to nature, and none on the experience of nature out of which the work of art proceeds. It was the latter that the Romantics rediscovered in a conscious, explicit way, and explored and reflected upon to a hitherto unknown degree. They had rediscovered the poetic experience of nature, or at least they had achieved a new awareness of it. They became conscious of that experience as a thing in itself, independent of its subsequent elaboration in a work, in something made. In doing so, they came to see this experience as a means of knowledge, immediate, experienced knowledge as opposed to discursive, abstract, scientific knowledge. Such immediate knowledge by experience of the thing known, by direct, lived contact, what Jacques Maritain calls a "savory" knowledge resulting from the "reverberation" of things in the soul, is very close to the mystical experience, and easily confused with it, with a direct knowledge by experience

---

and a nonrestrictive appositive could only be interpreted as unintentional, as an error.

[34] Lines 428-40.

of the Absolute. In the full early confidence of their new discovery, the Romantics attempted to find in the poetic experience
of nature a substitute for the mystical experience of God, without realizing that it would be only a substitute, an unsatisfactory
substitute, and that ultimately the attempt at substitution would
vitiate the poetic experience itself. Clearly the confusion in "Dejection" is not just metaphorical. It is not just that the relations
between the principals in the wedding are, to say the least, bizarre
(the groom being the father of the bride's father, as nearly as
one can tell), but that Coleridge is really supposing on the part of
the poet an impossible miracle, and it is no wonder he finds himself unable to perform it. Formerly, the soul had been *drawn*
to its "blest outstartings" by a highly animate nature, a nature
animated, in fact, by a totally immanent God. Now, in the very
words of Young, Coleridge is bemoaning the fact that his soul
is no longer "sent abroad"; but his account of nature now ex-
actly parallels that of Young, who, more consistently, affirms its
consequences.

A glance back at some of Coleridge's earlier poetic statements
concerning nature shows clearly what he had expected of the
poetic experience. In "Religious Musings" he says:

> And blest are they
> Who in this fleshly World, the elect of Heaven,
> Their strong eye darting through the deeds of men,
> Adore with steadfast unpresuming gaze
> Him Nature's essence, mind, and energy!
> And gazing, trembling, patiently ascend
> Treading beneath their feet all visible things
> As steps, that upward to their Father's throne
> Lead gradual—else nor glorified nor loved.[35]

God *is* the essence, mind, and energy of nature. From the doctrinal point of view, this is pantheism, or something virtually in-

[35] *Poems*, p. 111.

distinguishable from it, but what is important here is that the
end of the poetic experience of nature is not envisaged as the
creation of a work but as the mystical *experience* of God. Whether
pantheistic or not, the passage clearly indicates that the poetic
experience and the mystical experience are in the same line. A
later passage in the same poem is even more explicit.

> There is One mind, one omnipresent Mind,
> Omnific. His most holy name is love.
> Truth of subliming import! with the which
> Who feeds and saturates his constant soul,
> He from his small particular orbit flies
> With blest outstarting! From himself he flies,
> Stands in the sun, and with no partial gaze
> Views all creation; and he loves it all,
> And blesses it, and calls it very good!
> This is indeed to dwell with the Most High!
> Cherubs and rapture-trembling Seraphim
> Can press no nearer to the Almighty's throne.[36]

In 1795 Coleridge was asking himself,

> And what if all of animated nature
> Be but organic Harps diversely fram'd,
> That tremble into thought, as o'er them sweeps
> Plastic and vast, one intellectual breeze,
> At once the soul of each, and God of all?[37]

But it was only to be reproved for such "dim and unhallow'd"
thoughts by his young wife. In "The Destiny of Nations" we
find this passage:

> For what is Freedom, but the unfettered use
> Of all the powers which God for use had given?
> But chiefly this, him First, him Last to view
> Through meaner powers and secondary things

[36] *Ibid.*, p. 113. See in this book p. 123.
[37] *Poems*, p. 102, "The Eolian Harp."

> Effulgent, as through clouds that veil his blaze.
> For all that meets the bodily sense I deem
> Symbolical, one mighty alphabet
> For infant minds;[38]

Here are the "fair luminous clouds," but instead of issuing from the soul of the poet to envelop the earth, an inanimate cold earth, they *are* the earth, suffused with the light of God to the point of transparency. Here the doctrine is somewhat less than pantheistic, and amounts simply to saying something quite orthodox, a version of "The heavens declare the glory of God"; but a later passage reads:

> Glory to Thee Father of Earth and Heaven!
> All-conscious Presence of the Universe!
> Nature's vast ever-acting Energy!
> In will, in deed, Impulse of All to All![39]

In "This Lime-Tree Bower" (1797), Coleridge actually describes this kind of mystical experience of nature:

> So my friend
> Struck with deep joy may stand, as I have stood,
> Silent with swimming sense; yea, gazing round
> On the wide landscape, gaze till all doth seem
> Less gross than bodily; and of such hues
> As veil the Almighty Spirit, when yet he makes
> Spirits perceive his presence.[40]

Again the suggestion of the "fair luminous cloud." An earlier version of these lines, included by Coleridge in a letter to Thelwall, offers an even more direct and interesting comparison with "Dejection":

> 'Struck with the deepest calm of joy,' I stand
> Silent, with swimming sense; and gazing round

[38] *Ibid.*, p. 132.
[39] *Ibid.*, pp. 146-47.
[40] *Ibid.*, p. 180.

> On the wide landscape, gaze till all doth seem
> Less gross than bodily, a living Thing
> Which acts upon the mind and with such hues
> As clothe th' Almighty Spirit, where He makes
> Spirits perceive his presence![41]

Nature seems a "living Thing which acts upon the mind," and it acts by means of such "hues" as "clothe" the Almighty Spirit (compare the "wedding garment" of "Dejection"). The whole passage is something very like the description of an authentic mystical experience. The passage in the letter which these lines are used to illustrate is of particular interest:

I can *at times* feel strongly the beauties you describe, in themselves and for themselves; but more frequently *all things* appear *little,* all the knowledge that can be acquired child's play; the universe itself! what but an immense heap of *little* things? I can contemplate nothing but *parts,* and parts are all *little!* My mind feels as if it ached to behold and know something *great,* something *one* and *indivisible.* And it is only in the faith of that that rocks and waterfalls, mountains or caverns, give me the sense of sublimity or majesty! But in this faith *all things* counterfeit Infinity.

Already in 1797, nature in and for itself is only intermittently satisfying. It is only as a symbol of something "*one* and *indivisible*" that nature is significant, and it is not just as a symbol that he wants to conceive it but as an actual purveyor of the Absolute. He wants to "behold and know," here and now. The difference is all important, and we are reminded again of Baudelaire's "revealed paradise."[42] As he makes clear later on in the same poem, there is no doubt about the impetus furnished by nature:

> Henceforth I shall know
> That Nature ne'er deserts the wise and pure;
> No plot so narrow, be but Nature there,

[41] *Letters,* LXXV (October 16, 1797), I, 228.
[42] See in this book p. 116.

No waste so vacant, but may well employ
Each faculty of sense, and keep the heart
Alive to Love and Beauty![43]

Man's contribution to the total experience, important as it is, is negative: by being wise and pure, he prepares himself to receive the message of Nature, to be quickened by its contact. In "Dejection" purity is still a requisite for "Joy"; but instead of Nature's keeping the heart alive to love and beauty, it is the soul's self-produced joy that gives life to Nature.

In "The Nightingale" (1798), he goes so far as to inveigh against the pathetic fallacy involved in man's reading his own feelings into nature instead of surrendering to its influxes:

In Nature there is nothing melancholy.
But some night-wandering man whose heart was pierced
With the remembrance of a grievous wrong,
Or slow distemper, or neglected love,
(And so, poor wretch! filled all things with himself,
And made all gentle sounds tell back the tale
Of his own sorrow) he, and such as he,
First named these notes a melancholy strain.[44]

He is speaking here of the

Poet who hath been building up the rhyme
When he had better far have stretched his limbs
Beside a brook in mossy forest-dell,
By sun or moon-light, to the influxes
Of shapes and sounds and shifting elements
Surrendering his whole spirit, of his song
And of his fame forgetful! so his fame
Should share in Nature's immortality,
A venerable thing! and so his song
Should make all Nature lovelier, and itself
Be loved like Nature![45]

[43] *Poems,* p. 181.
[44] *Ibid.,* p. 264.
[45] *Ibid.,* pp. 264-65 (quoted in this book p. 99).

This poem offers an eloquent description of the poetic enter-
prise, emphasizing the necessity for the poetic experience to precede artistic elaboration, if the latter is not to be empty and false.
It is significant that it was written in 1798, at the height of Coleridge's poetic career. It is surely true that in a sense the poet must
be forgetful of his song, that he must allow the experience of
nature to have its way with him, that a kind of genuine cogni-
tion must precede the work of the artist. It is of this experience
that the Romantics achieved a fresh awareness. Their danger was
of forgetting that the experience, this reverberation in the receptive soul, was by its nature ordered to artistic creation, to expression in a work, and was not, like the mystical experience properly
so called, an experience complete in itself. The danger was in-
tensified by their tendency toward pantheism—if God is completely immanent in nature, then the poetic experience *is* identical with the mystical experience, and poems would result from
it only *per accidens,* by a kind of super-abundance, as in the case
of the mystics, for whom the artistic recreation of their experience in which they sometimes indulge is by no means necessary to
the completion thereof. Here in this poem, far from being cold
and inanimate, Nature is lovable and immortal; and there is no
suggestion that the poet is responsible for this fact.

Only a year later we find the first indication of disillusion, in
the "Lines Written in the Album at Elbingrode" (1799):

> I moved on
> In low and languid mood: for I had found
> That outward forms, the loftiest, still receive
> Their finer influence from the Life within;—
> Fair cyphers else: fair, but of import vague
> Or unconcerning, where the heart not finds
> History or prophecy of friend, or child,
> Or father, or the venerable name
> Of our adoréd country![46]

[46] *Ibid.,* pp. 315-16. See in this book pp. 106-8.

But he is not yet ready to make the categorical statement of "Dejection"; instead, he says:

> Stranger, these impulses
> Blame thou not lightly; nor will I profane
> That man's sublimer spirit, who can feel
> That God is everywhere! the God who framed
> Mankind to be one mighty family,
> Himself our Father, and the World our Home.[47]

When we read the fourth stanza of "Dejection" against the background of these earlier passages, it is clear that the stanza is not just an objective description of the poetic relation between man and nature, of a particular conception of that relation at which Coleridge had arrived in the abstract, but it is also the reflection of a metamorphosis in his own experience. It constitutes a kind of recantation of his earlier beliefs concerning the poetic experience. As a matter of fact, this is evident from the very cast of the language. Its tone, from the opening exclamatory address through to the end, is one of protestation. It is in our life *alone* that Nature lives. There is something deliberately negative rather than merely neutral about "that inanimate cold world," which is all that is "allowed / To the poor loveless ever-anxious crowd." In the next line there is hardly more than one real stress, that upon "it*self*": "Ah! from the soul it*self* must issue forth"; and this is repeated with variation three lines further on in the stanza. In the line following that one, the idea is repeated a second time: the sweet and potent voice is of the soul's *own* birth. As has been seen, Coleridge is not content with a single image to represent the soul's contribution to the poetic transaction, but piles image upon image. It is a light, a glory, a fair luminous cloud, and later a sweet and potent voice. This multiplication of images is at least in part, no doubt, just an-

[47] *Poems*, p. 316.

other expression of urgency, or insistence in the repudiation of his former faith in the influxes of nature. But it may also result from his feeling that the light symbol, for him the perennial symbol of the poetic experience, is no longer adequate or fully appropriate. This light had always previously been an atmosphere in which the poet *found* himself, an atmosphere produced by the contact between the poet and nature, not something produced or secreted as it were by the poet himself. It is somehow more natural to think of the poet, the soul, producing a sound, a voice, than producing a light. Yet the light image is still necessary, because the poet is seen as clothing nature with a new appearance, as a result of which he can "behold" things of higher worth in her.

A sizable portion of Coleridge's poetry is explicitly concerned with the elucidation of the poetic experience. Probably never before the Romantic period had so much poetry been written about poetry. Coleridge's critical observations and analyses of it are surely among the keenest and most profound in the language, and it is for this reason among others that he is sometimes credited with being the father of modern criticism.[48] Further, we may agree with Richards[49] that Coleridge, like Wordsworth, seems to alternate between the projective and the realist views of the poetic experience, emphasizing now one and now the other, because on the level of normal poetic experience and production the two doctrines are not in opposition to one another. The poetic experience is an experience of *contact* between the poet and nature, and both the poet and nature contribute to its creative virtualities, and both come to be known through the product. Both emphases are valid and important in the effort to characterize what is, after all, a difficult experience to communicate.

[48] See T. S. Eliot, "The Frontiers of Criticism," *Sewanee Review*, LXIV (1956), 527.

[49] *Coleridge on Imagination*, p. 146.

But at the time of "Dejection" Coleridge is assuming the projective view to the exclusion of the realist view, and he is doing it not because he did not have a remarkably refined and profound explicit conception of the authentic experience, but because in the course of his development as a poet he came to burden it with an invalid expectation that vitiated his own experience and led him into confusion and contradiction.

In the following chapter this development will be examined in the light of an aesthetic formulation which might at first glance seem peculiarly ill-adapted to the task of illuminating the experience of an anti-French, anti-Catholic admirer of German Idealism: the formulation of the French, Catholic Thomists, Jacques and Raïssa Maritain. Such a confrontation may be justified on a number of grounds. In a general way, it seems often to be true that the sympathetic application of foreign criteria to a body of thought throws into understandable relief certain obscurities which the light of analysis in its own indigenous terms has failed to reach—and this even when a very minimum of affinity exists. But it is possible in the present case to discover much more than a necessary minimum of affinity.

This should not be surprising. If Coleridge has turned out to be a peculiarly unsatisfactory philosopher in professional terms, the reason is probably that in philosophy he was, however learned, essentially an amateur, and an amateur of a *practical* sort. It may be true that all of the great philosophers have been amateurs of just this sort, men seeking anywhere and everywhere for formulations to render their experience understandable, and bearable; though only the very greatest of them have finally resisted the temptation to turn professional in order to complete the "system." Only the very greatest have achieved a considerable expanse of consistency without the aid of any self-conscious, professional scruples about consistency and without any doctoring of the evidence in order to achieve it. Thus it could be said that Coleridge is in the authentic line of great philosophers if we look to his motives and to his manner of proceeding. He simply did not achieve a sufficiently wide expanse of consistency to place him among the giants.[50]

But for our present purposes what this means, this systematizing eclecticism, is that it is not surprising to find affinities between Coleridge's thought, or his way of thinking and feeling, and that of anyone else who has his eye on similar objects. It would not be a very useful experiment to view Coleridge through the lenses provided by a great many conventional Thomist manuals which concern themselves at some point with the philosophy of art; but the Maritains are distinguished by their sensitive attention to the data of poetic experience, particularly modern poetic experience, while bringing to bear upon these data the formidable and delicate instruments offered by St. Thomas. In Coleridge's attempt to formulate his experience in relation to a very different set of metaphysical principles from those underlying the Maritains' analyses, he arrived at a number of conclusions strikingly similar to theirs—enough to suggest that their analyses of the poetic experience might be more than casually relevant to an understanding of Coleridge's problems.

---

[50] See Abrams, *The Mirror and the Lamp,* pp. 114 ff., on Coleridge's perennial concern that his critical principles follow from metaphysical first principles.

An analogy may be drawn between philosophers and poets in this matter—we have the great amateurs, who, however learned in the ways of poetry, write only as far as their vision goes, but then it goes very far; we have the professionals, who write complete epics, with all the conventional appurtenances, and carefully "reflecting a culture"; and we have the more or less great amateurs, whose vision is less wide, but very clear, and who do not cheat. I would venture to place Coleridge as a poet among this third group.

V

THE ROMANTIC
ÉCHEC

In the foregoing discussion a good deal of use has been made of
passages from Coleridge's poems as evidence of developments in
his intellectual and emotional life, centering upon the poem "De
jection" as a document in his spiritual biography. The more or
less direct biographical interpretation of poetry is full of dangers
—to the poetry and to the biography. Certainly it can sometimes
be, as Warren says,

the equivalent of the fallacy of *argumentum ad hominem* in logic,
and of the fallacy in aesthetics of assuming identity of the material
and the thing created from the material, for it overlooks the symbolic
extensions and the universalizing and normalizing process always in-
herent in the creative act.[1]

But the danger is not an absolute one in either direction, in interpreting the poetry by means of the life or the life by means
of the poetry, if the interpreter does his best *not* to overlook the
symbolic extensions, and if his best is good enough.

It might also be observed that the danger varies with different
poets, and even with different poems of the same poet. It should
probably be accepted as a matter of definition that, to be recognized as a product of the "creative act," a poem must always involve *some* symbolic extension, since the most accurate and sensitive
reporting is not, as such, poetry. The raw materials must undergo

[1] "A Poem of Pure Imagination," p. 73.

to *some* extent a normalizing and universalizing process, although neoclassical requirements in this direction are often exaggerated. But poets and poems differ widely in these respects, and require very different readings. There is not, for example, the same degree of symbolic extension in "Religious Musings" and in *The Ancient Mariner*. Perhaps the critic's first job is to estimate the degree of symbolic extension in the poem he is about to interpret. Coleridge sometimes explicitly recognized the difference among his own poems in this respect. He said of his sonnet, "On Receiving a Letter Informing Me of the Birth of a Son" (1796) that "This sonnet puts in no claim to poetry (indeed as a composition I think so little of them [this and the other sonnet on the same subject] that I neglected to repeat them to you) but it is a most faithful picture of my feelings on a very interesting event."[2] This remark alone suggests that he agrees that symbolic extension is indispensable to poetry. In quoting lines 87-93 of "Dejection" to Tom Wedgwood, he says, "I give you these lines for the Truth and not for the Poetry."[3] And in quoting the whole of Stanza VI to Sotheby he says that he "thus expressed the thought in language more forcible than harmonious."[4]

But although these considerations are ample to justify a careful biographical use of Coleridge's poems, there is something more important to be learned from them. It seems to be true that some Romantic poets more frequently indulged in direct transcription, without the symbolic extension indispensable to the creative act, than did the Metaphysical or the Augustan poets, for example, and this seriously hurt the quality of much of their poetry. And yet they *were* true poets, capable of brilliant and profound symbolic extensions, as capable as their predecessors—

[2] *Poems*, p. 153*n*.
[3] *Unpublished Letters*, I, 215 (October 20, 1802).
[4] *Letters*, I, 378-79 (July 19, 1802).

some "new critics" seemed for a time to be almost totally blinded to this fact by the large volume of apparently direct transcription of personal feelings to be found in their work. This tendency of the Romantic poets can be accounted for in part, as a simple reaction against the exaggerated artificialities in style which characterized much late neoclassical poetry. Wordsworth said that in order to defend the theory of poetry which *Lyrical Ballads* exemplified, "it would be necessary to give a full account of the present state of public taste, and to determine how far this taste is healthy or depraved."[5] The new poets' inclination to stick to nature unadorned represented a revolt against "arbitrary and capricious habits of expression,"[6] what Coleridge called "thoughts *translated* into the language of poetry."[7]

Neither Wordsworth nor Coleridge was in any theoretical doubt concerning the necessity of symbolic extension—more simply, of art—in poetry. Coleridge lists as one of the promises of genius "the choice of subjects very remote from the private interests and circumstances of the writer himself."[8] And he is quite clear on the subject in explaining the first impact of Wordsworth's poetry upon him:

It was not however the freedom from false taste, whether as to common defects, or to those more properly his own, which made so unusual an impression on my feelings immediately, and subsequently on my judgment. It was the union of deep feeling with profound thought; the fine balance of truth in observing, with the imaginative faculty in modifying the objects observed; and above all the original gift of spreading the tone, the *atmosphere*, and with it the depth and height of the ideal world around forms, incidents, and situations, of

---

[5] Preface to the Second Edition of *Lyrical Ballads*, in *The Poetical Works of Wordsworth*, ed. by T. Hutchinson (London: Oxford University Press, 1932), p. 934.

[6] *Ibid.*, p. 935. Cf. *Biographia Literaria*, II, 11-12.

[7] *Biographia Literaria*, II, 14.

[8] *Ibid.*

which, for the common view, custom had bedimmed all lustre, had
dried up the sparkle and the dew drops.[9]

These passages, and others that could be cited, bear ample witness
to the fact that Coleridge was in no danger of ignoring in principle the proper autonomy of the work of art.[10]

But at the same time it is impossible to read what Wordsworth
and Coleridge have to say about the poetic experience, or to read
their poems, without getting the impression that the poetic activity exercised a function in their lives which was somehow supra-
artistic, that they cherished the poetic experience as fulfilling some
peculiarly personal need, to which the creation of poems was
more or less incidental. They certainly speak of it with an accent
decidedly different from that of their predecessors. As Albert
Béguin remarks concerning Karl Philipp Moritz,

each of these attitudes is a response to the problem of his own life,
the problem of the self which on the one hand seeks by means of the
imagination to plunge itself into a reality in which it can realize all its
potentialities, and on the other hand resents everything external to it
as constituting a stifling prison.[11]

And we might also say of Coleridge (and more confidently of
Wordsworth) as Béguin says of Moritz:

His most beautiful passages are those in which he feels nature to be
completely symbolic of his feelings, either when, momentarily freed
from his habitual anguish, he achieves a kind of beneficent melan-

---

[9] *Ibid.*, I, 59. See also II, 16: "images, however beautiful, though faithfully
copied from nature, and as accurately represented in words, do not of themselves
characterize the poet. They become proofs of original genius only as far as they
are modified by a predominant passion; or by associated thoughts or images
awakened by that passion; or when they have the effect of reducing multitude to
unity, or succession to an instant; or lastly, when a human and intellectual life
is transferred to them from the poet's own spirit."

[10] Abrams, *The Mirror and the Lamp*, pp. 116-24, discusses in a very illuminating way Coleridge's views on the tension between spontaneity and order in
poetic composition.

[11] *L'Ame Romantique*, I, 91.

choly, or on the contrary, when the countryside tragically reflects his
own internal drama to him. . . .[12]

Coleridge's own expression of regret at the apparent loss of his
poetic powers and most notably the poetic expression of regret
in "Dejection," have an almost agonizing ring, which might
strike one as inappropriate. In view of his repeated statements that
he avoided poetic composition and took refuge in abstruse researches because the poetic experience aroused too painful feelings, it is curious, as we have noted, that what he is complaining
of in "Dejection" is precisely an *absence* of feeling,

> A Grief without a pang, void, dark and drear,
> A stifling, drowsy, unimpassioned Grief
> That finds no natural outlet, no Relief
> In word, or sigh, or tear—

a "heartless mood." And lines in the original version, later
omitted, state explicitly that this had become a chronic, not just
a momentary state of mind with him:

> This, Sara! well thou know'st,
> Is that sore evil, which I dread the most,
> And oft'nest suffer![13]

He is complaining primarily of the loss of an *experience*. His
delicate powers of observation are unimpaired, but his responses
are atrophied. He gazes "with how blank an eye," he sees, not
feels the beauties of nature. It is only late in the poem, in Stanza
VI, that he alludes to the fact that this suspends his "shaping
spirit of Imagination," his artistic creativity, his ability to write
poems.

It is this conscious distinction between the poetic experience and
the artistic elaboration of it which is of utmost importance in
considering the Romantic poets, and which renders the biographi-

---

[12] *Ibid.,* p. 76.
[13] Whalley, *Coleridge and Sara Hutchinson,* pp. 155-56.

cal interpretation of their poetry peculiarly relevant. In order to understand the part this distinction played, not only as the source of some of the really unique contributions of the Romantic poets to the fund of human sensibility, but also as a source at the same time of their artistic and personal tragedies, it will be necessary to examine in some detail the nature of the poetic experience and especially its relation to the actual composition of poems, making use in doing this of some of Jacques Maritain's insights into these matters.

Professor Maritain points out that the "poetic experience" *per se* may be distinguished from the artistic elaboration in which it normally issues; but at the same time he attempts to explain why this experience is normally directed toward creation, toward making, rather than toward knowing (as are "abstruse researches"), or toward objective union with the object known (as in the mystical experience, or, on a different level, the experience of human love). He says that

in order to answer this question it would be necessary to turn one's attention first toward *subjectivity* as such [it is clearly of some disease of his "subjectivity" that Coleridge is complaining in "Dejection"]. Subjectivity truly and properly so called begins only with personality, or rather the two are aspects of the same thing. Subjectivity is intimately connected with the privileges of spirituality and of immanence proper to the personality itself. A subjectivity is a spiritual subsistence and existence, which are radically alive, sources of the superexistence of knowledge and the superexistence of love; and if in the case of these activities all specification comes from the object, all the vitality, on the other hand, and all the vital productivity come from the subjectivity itself.[14]

We may pause here to recall Coleridge's lines:

> I may not hope from outward forms to win
> The Passion and the Life, whose fountains are within!

[14] *Situation of Poetry*, p. 72.

And:

> We receive but what we give,
> And in our Life alone does Nature live:
> Ours is her wedding garment, ours her shroud!
> And would we aught behold of higher worth. . . .
>   Ah! from the soul itself must issue forth
> A light, a glory, a fair luminous cloud
>   Enveloping the Earth—
> And from the soul itself must there be sent
>   A sweet and potent voice, of its own birth,
> Of all sweet sounds the life and element![15]

In other words, Coleridge's subjectivity is no longer furnishing the passion and the life. He is suffering from a lapse of what Maritain calls the vital productivity, which is characteristic of subjectivity by its very nature:

A subjectivity appears thus, by virtue of its most deeply-rooted properties, as a center of a universe unto itself, a universe of productive vitality and spiritual emanation.[16]

What then is the relation between this subjectivity, this productive vitality, and the specifying object, or Nature, which characterizes the poetic experience, as distinguished from other experiences of the external world, and which causes it to issue in a *making,* a creation, rather than in a conceptual *knowing,* or an objective *union?* What peculiar kind of contact between the subjectivity and nature constitutes a poetic experience? Maritain first distinguishes experiences like the Hindu mystical contemplation of the "self," which is attained through progressive ascetic divorce from the external world, and which issues in silence, from the poetic experience, which issues in creation:

if by a trick, by some kind of detour of the spirit, an experience of the self succeeds in a supra- or para-conceptual way in grasping the sub-

---

[15] *Poems,* p. 365.
[16] *Situation of Poetry,* pp. 72-73.

ject and its intimate being, transferred to the state of an object, of a terminus of contemplative union, this experience will not constitute a poetic experience.

But, he goes on to say,

if an experience of the self by the self grasps the subject *as subject,* that is to say, in its quality of being radically and in living act the principle of productive vitality and spiritual emanation, then such an experience will be by that very fact a fecundation, as it were, of that very productivity.[17]

Under what circumstances does this happen? Under what circumstances does the subject grasp itself in that way *as subject* and no longer as object? When does it, as it were, catch itself in the act of being a subject? Obviously not when it is directly concentrating on itself by an act of reflection, observing itself as an object, but rather,

such a grasp of the substance of the subject can only take place in a non-conceptual or non-logical mode, hence in an essentially obscure manner, *at the very instant when some reality from the universe outside is grasped by mode of affective connaturality, in an intuitive emotion in which the universe and the subject are revealed together to the subject,* as if by a beam of darkness. For it is in awakening to the world, it is in obscurely grasping some substantial secret in things, that the soul of man obscurely grasps itself.

That is the poetic experience or poetic knowledge, in which the subjectivity is not grasped as object by an explicit reflection, but as source and *in actu exercitu,* in the very process of grasping things by virtue of their resonance in the subject.[18]

Coleridge had long been aware of this experience as a distinct phenomenon, a contact between the soul and nature in which the things of nature are received into the soul of the poet in its most active depths of sensibility. Concerning this sensibility, he is reported by his friend John Frere to have said that

[17] *Ibid.,* p. 73.
[18] *Ibid.* (italics mine).

Poetry is the highest activity of the mind; all the powers are in a state of equilibrium and equally energetic, the knowledge of individual existence is forgotten, the man is out of himself and exists in all things[19]

Raïssa Maritain observes that poetry "is born in man in his deepest self, there where all his faculties originate."[20] It involves, she says, "a certain withdrawal . . . a certain sleep of the faculties . . . a certain interior silence, which disposes the poet sometimes to divine influences, sometimes to the keen perception of natural causes"; and she quotes St. Thomas:

When the soul is abstracted from the sense, it becomes more apt to receive the influence of spiritual substances and also to follow the subtle movements which are born in the imagination from the impression of natural causes, something which is very difficult when it is absorbed in sensible things.[21]

Here we may find echoes not only of Coleridge but also of Wordsworth's "emotion recollected in tranquility," as well as the overweening ambitions the Romantics conceived for poetry.

A further characteristic of the experience is what we might call its peculiar emotional charge. In the *Lay Sermon,* in distinguishing poetry from science, Coleridge speaks of

that pleasurable emotion, that peculiar state and degree of excitement, which arises in the poet himself in the act of composition;—and in order to understand this, we must combine a more than ordinary sympathy with the object, emotions, or incidents contemplated by the poet, consequent on a more than common sensibility, with a more than ordinary activity of the mind in respect of fancy and imagination. Hence is produced a more vivid reflection of the truths of nature and of the human heart, united with a constant activity modifying and correcting these truths by that sort of pleasurable emotion, which

---

[19] Quoted by Armour and Howes, *Coleridge the Talker*, pp. 213-14.
[20] *Situation of Poetry*, p. 6.
[21] *Ibid.*, pp. 19-20.

the exertion of all our faculties give in a certain degree; but which
can only be felt in perfection under the full play of those powers of
mind, which are spontaneous rather than voluntary, and in which the
effort required bears no proportion to the activity enjoyed.[22]

Concerning this "pleasurable emotion" which takes over to mod-
ify and correct the objective content of the poetic experience,
Mme Maritain quotes an illuminating passage from Béguin:

At the height of the poetic experience the frontiers between an exterior
and an interior world disappear; all is image, offered to the free disposition of a spirit which recomposes according to its own wish the
order of everything given. The poet remakes from what is given him
a universe suiting his own exigencies, according to his pleasure, con-
forming himself only to the law of that euphoria which is aroused in
him by this rhythm, that sonorous echo, that association of forms and
colors.[23]

The result of this activation, this peculiar contact between the
soul and things which constitutes the poetic experience, is, on
the one hand, that the things of nature reveal ordinarily un-
noticed correspondences, among themselves and with the soul.
Coleridge's virtually countless statements concerning the recon-
ciliation of opposites, and his whole doctrine of the imagination
as a "coadunating" power, bear upon this point. As Wordsworth
puts it in Book II of *The Prelude* (lines 382-86):

> The song would speak
> Of that interminable building reared
> By observation of affinities
> In objects where no brotherhood exists
> To passive minds.

On the other hand, by this activation of the faculties, by this
reverberation of objects received into the soul, the soul is also

22 *Complete Works*, VI, 183.
23 Maritain, *Situation of Poetry*, p. 30.

revealed to itself. Concerning this knowledge of the subject by itself, Maritain observes that

> It is an experience at the same time of the world and of the subjectivity, in which, to speak the scholastic jargon, the content most immediately grasped is the world, the content *most principally* (and most secretly) grasped is the subjectivity.[24]

Coleridge seems to be noticing the same thing in his own experience when he says that

> In looking at objects of Nature while I am thinking, as at yonder moon dim-glimmering through the dewy window-pane, I seem rather to be seeking, as it were *asking* for, a symbolical language for something within me that already and forever exists, than observing anything new. Even when that latter is the case, yet still I have always an obscure feeling as if that new phenomena were the dim awaking of a forgotten or hidden truth of my own nature.[25]

In the light of "Dejection" and the poems preceding it, it is natural that Coleridge should choose "yonder moon dim-glimmering" as an object of nature to furnish a symbolical language for something within him; and we should immediately recognize this as a description of the poetic experience. Béguin remarks concerning Moritz that his nature descriptions

> [bear] the mark of a completely new feeling toward nature; its forms are no longer anything but symbols of an interior reality, beauty takes second place, the visual spectacle serves as an expression of events in the soul. . . .[26]

This would serve very well as a characterization of the use of nature in most of Coleridge's so-called conversational poems, although Béguin might seem to do less than justice to the complexity of the experience in saying that the forms of nature are

---

24 *Situation of Poetry*, pp. 73-74.
25 *Anima Poetae*, p. 136.
26 *L'Ame Romantique*, I, 76.

not "anything but" symbols of an interior reality, unless we were
sure that he had in mind something like Coleridge's definition
of a symbol as partaking of the reality it manifests.

Maritain makes the point that these knowledges, of the object
and of the self, originate in a felt, experienced contact rather than
in discursive reasoning, as is the case with scientific knowledge.
The Scholastics distinguished such knowledge from scientific
knowledge by the term "knowledge by connaturality," more specifically (since there is an element of connaturality in all knowledge), "knowledge by affective connaturality." Poetic intuition,
Maritain says,

takes place by affective connaturality, by virtue of the resonance of
that which is most existent and most concrete in things in that which
is most existent and concrete in the subject; . . . it proceeds, not from
some tense reflective asceticism against the grain of nature, tending
toward a kind of metaphysical death or release, but on the contrary
from a natural and eminently spontaneous movement of the soul
which is seeking itself in communing with things by means of the
sense imbued with intelligence.[27]

Coleridge gives us a metaphorical image of this connaturality
between things and the mind which is at the source of the poetic
experience in one of the notations collected in the *Anima Poetae*
for the year 1804:

Thought and reality are, as it were, two distinct corresponding sounds,
of which no man can say positively which is the voice and which
the echo.

Oh, the beautiful fountain or natural well at Upper Stowey! The
images of the weeds which hung down from its sides appear as
plants growing up, straight and upright, among the water-weeds that
really grow from the bottom of the well, and so vivid was the image,

---

[27] *Situation of Poetry*, p. 76. Concerning the "spontaneous" character of this
movement of the soul, compare Coleridge's statement from the *Lay Sermon*,
quoted here p. 160.

that for some moments, and not till after I had disturbed the water, did I perceive that their roots were not neighbours, and they side-by-side companions. So ever, then I said, so are the happy man's thoughts and things, his ideas and impressions.[28]

In his *Philosophical Lectures,* speaking of Pythagoras, he uses the term "connaturality" in connection with the "creative and organizing powers":

the very powers which in men reflect and contemplate, are in essence the same as those powers which in nature produce the objects contemplated. This position did indeed appear to be deducible from that of the Ionic school, I mean that of Thales, that there is no action but from like on like, that no substance or being essentially dissimilar could possibly be made sensible of each other's existence or in any way act thereon.

This involves an essential—I know not how I can avoid using a pedantic word—HOMOGENEITY and connaturality—a sameness of the concipient and the conceptum, of the idea and the law corresponding to the idea.[29]

One other discussion of this point occurs in the essay, "On the Principles of Genial Criticism," which has already been cited in connection with Coleridge's conception of love. In distinguishing between goodness and beauty, he says:

The GOOD consists in congruity of a thing with the laws of reason and the nature of the will, and its fitness to determine the latter to actualize the former, and it is always discursive. The BEAUTIFUL arises from the perceived harmony of an object, whether of sight or sound, with the inborn and constitutive rules of the judgment and imagination: and it is always intuitive. As light to the eye, even such is beauty to the mind, which cannot but have complacency in whatever is perceived as preconfigured to its living faculties. Hence the Greeks called a beautiful object καλόν, quasi καλοῦν, i.e. *calling* on the

[28] p. 143.
[29] p. 114.

soul, which receives it instantly, and welcomes it as something connatural.[30]

Earlier in the same essay he characterizes the beautiful as that
"which is naturally consonant with our senses by the pre-estab-
lished harmony between nature and the human mind."[31]

But why is this experience, this resonance of things in the soul
through which the poet comes to know something of things and
something of himself, why is this experience, as Maritain puts
it, "radically factive or formative," naturally realizable only in
a *work?* Because, Maritain explains,

being inseparable from the productivity of the spirit (owing to the
fact that the connaturality which awakens it actuates the subject as
subject, or as center of productive vitality and spiritual emanation), it
nevertheless cannot (because it attains the real only as buried in the
subjectivity itself, and therefore nonconceptualizable) expand in a
concept produced *ad intra,* in a mental word. Consequently, it can
issue only in a work *ad extra.*

It appears then that the radical tendency of the poetic experience
toward creation *ad extra,* in other words its belonging by origin in
the line of art, must be related to its essential connection with the
actual exercise of the subjectivity. . . .[32]

Coleridge recognizes this natural inseparability of poetic knowledge and artistic elaboration or creativity when he says that

Every work of Fine Art is a Language, the essence of which is that it
cannot be divided from the meaning (the Mind) it transfers, without
ipso facto ceasing to be a Language—So here the Product is inseparable from the Productivity—for Life is so definable—[33]

The converse surely follows, that the Productivity is inseparable
from the Product and fully realizes itself only in the work made.

[30] *Biographia Literaria,* II, 243.
[31] *Ibid.,* p. 233.
[32] *Situation of Poetry,* p. 74.
[33] In T. M. Raysor, "Unpublished Fragments on Aesthetics by Samuel Taylor
Coleridge," *Studies in Philology* (1925), p. 529.

It is important that up to this point in the characterization of the poetic act, following the conceptions of the Maritains and Béguin, we have found corroboration in Coleridge's descriptions of his own experience and in his pronouncements as a critic concerning the nature of the poetic experience. For it is at this point that we can begin to see one of the perils to which they find the poet is exposed, and to which Coleridge himself seems to have fallen victim. But it is clear that for this to happen to him, he must have experienced and conceived of the poetic act in something like these terms, since the peril in question involves a confusion describable in just these terms concerning the nature and efficacy of the poetic act.

After discussing the euphoria under whose influence the poet operates at the height of the poetic experience, that pleasurable emotion which Coleridge says "can only be felt in perfection under the full play of those powers of mind, which are spontaneous rather than voluntary,"[34] Béguin says:

But, at this sovereign point, the spirit ceases to consider itself as the author of the song in which it finds its felicity; it seems to perceive a voice which is no longer its own. That which speaks is not itself but another *who stirs in the depths,* in a symphony which responds to the stroke of its bow.[35]

Here is where the poetic experience and mysticism seem to touch. The poet becomes, in the most literal sense, prophet; all poetry, the production of which is incidental, a species of divine revelation. At one point Coleridge was willing to say that "all truth is a species of revelation."[36] The poet becomes an instrument, an Eolian harp, played upon by the winds of the Spirit. At this point the poet "can also," says Maritain, "by going against the

---

34 See in this book p. 161.
35 Quoted by Raïssa Maritain, *Situation of Poetry,* p. 31.
36 *Letters,* I, 352 (to Thos. Poole, March 23, 1801).

nature of things, turn this intuition aside from its operative ends, and seek by a kind of violence, and to his sorrow . . . to turn it into a pure knowledge."[37] But for this to happen, it is necessary that the poet be explicitly conscious of the poetic *experience* in isolation from its natural devolment into a work of artistic creation. Coleridge was keenly aware of this distinction.

Maritain offers some illuminating suggestions concerning the historical process through which such an explicit consciousness of the poetic experience came into being. He calls attention to the fact that until quite recently the word "poetry," *poiesis,* was roughly synonymous with what we call *art,* "the activity of the working reason." There was no conscious distinction between the experience out of which the work of art grows and the actual process of materially creating the work; then

One might say that piercing and boring through metaphysical layers the word poetry has little by little traversed the body of the poetic work and arrived at its soul, where it has opened out into the spiritual realm. This phenomenon will not appear very surprising if one admits that poetry has only recently begun (*poets,* that is, have only recently begun) to become self-conscious in an explicit and deliberate way (and this process will never have finished).[38]

Some of Coleridge's "definitions" of poetry reflect just such a consciousness and appreciation of the dignity of poetry. "All fine arts are different species of poetry," he says. "The same spirit speaks to the mind through different senses by manifestations of itself appropriate to each."[39] And again:

I am preparing an essay on the Connection of Statuary and Sculpture with Religion: the origin of statuary as a fine art, that is, as a form or species of Poesy (which I distinguish from poetry as a genus from one of its species).[40]

[37] *Situation of Poetry,* p. 75.
[38] *Ibid.,* p. 37.
[39] "Essays on the Fine Arts," *Biographia Literaria,* II, 220-21.
[40] *Unpublished Letters,* II, 336 (to John Flaxman, January 24, 1825).

His most extended statement concerning the dignity of poetry
is to be found in a letter to Joseph Cottle:

The common end of all *narrative,* nay, of *all,* Poems is to convert a
series into a *Whole*: to make those events, which in real or imagined
History move on in a *strait* Line, assume to our Understandings a
circular motion—the snake with it's Tail in it's mouth. Hence indeed
the almost flattering and yet appropriate term, Poesy—i.e. *Poiēsis*=
making. Doubtless, to his *his* [sic] eye, which alone comprehends all
Past and all Future in one eternal Present, what to our short sight
appears strait is but a part of the great Cycle—just as the calm Sea
to us *appears* level, tho' it be indeed only a part of a *globe.* Now what
the Globe is in Geography, *miniaturing* in order to *manifest* the
Truth, such is a Poem to that Image of God, which we were created
with, and which still seeks that Unity, or Revelation of the *One* in
and by the *Many,* which reminds it, that tho' in order to be an individual Being it must go forth *from* God, yet as the *re*ceding from him
is to *pro*ceed towards Nothingness and Privation, it must still at
every step turn back toward him in order to *be* at all— Now, a straight
Line, continuously retracted forms of necessity a circular orbit. Now
God's Will and Word *cannot* be frustrated. His aweful *Fiat* was with
ineffable awefulness applied to Man, when all things and all living
Things, himself (as a mere animal) included, were called forth by the
Universal—*Let there be*—and then the Breath of the Eternal super-
added to make an *immortal* Spirit—immortality being, as the author
of the 'Wisdom of Solomon' profoundly expresses it, the only possible
Reflex or Image of Eternity. The Immortal Finite is the contracted
Shadow of the Eternal Infinite. Therefore nothingness or *Death,* to
which we move as we recede from God and the Word, *cannot* be
nothing; but that tremendous medium between nothing and true
Being, which Scripture and inmost Reason present most, most horrible! I have said this to shew you the connection between things in
themselves comparatively trifling, and things the most important, by
their derivation from common sources.[41]

The poem is a miniature of the human soul, reminding it that it
is an image of God, to whom it must return. Here poetry has,

[41] *Unpublished Letters,* II, 128-29 (to Joseph Cottle, March 7, 1815).

as Maritain puts it, opened out into the spiritual realm, although at the time of this writing, in 1815, there is no suggestion of separation from its operational ends. Maritain goes about the matter somewhat differently, but the effect is strikingly similar:

> The Mind, the subsisting Mind, can fully realize in God alone, in the pure Act alone, the fundamental exigencies of its nature and give birth to *another self* at once substantial and personal, to a Word which shall be truly a Son. In the Holy Trinity alone do we see the coincidence of the two functions which everywhere else are separate, the utterance of the Word and the generation of the Son, the Mind ending in a subsisting goal, in which the integrity of its own nature becomes substantially merged.
>
> Well! We too, feeble though our mind be (it is on the lowest rung of spirits), ought to share in the nature of mind. For this reason the mind, despite the manifold defects peculiar to our species, strives to engender in us, is anxious to produce, not only the inner Word, the idea remaining inside us, but a work at once material and spiritual, like ourselves, with something of our soul over and above.
>
> This requirement of the mind explains the presence of artists in our midst.
>
> And you see that to establish fully the dignity and nobility of art, we have found it necessary to go back as far as the mystery of the Trinity.[42]

Concerning the process of poetry's becoming progressively conscious of itself, Maritain maintains that it exemplifies

> one of the great laws of the historical development of the human being, and . . . is related to a property of activities of a spiritual order. The distinctive property of spirit is to be able, the ancients said, to return entirely upon itself, to accomplish a perfect reflection, the essential here being not the turning back, but the grasp, the penetration of the self by the self, which is integral to it. Reflexivity is essential to the spirit, which thus grasps itself by means of itself and

[42] *Art and Scholasticism* (New York: Scribners, 1930), p. 97.

penetrates itself. Thence the general importance, for everything concerning culture, of the phenomenon of becoming self-conscious.[43]

The generation to which Coleridge belonged, the Romantics, can on one level be best understood as having accomplished one of the major steps in this continuing process of poetry's becoming self-conscious. There have been theories of poetry as far back as we know, but up to the end of the eighteenth century the emphasis had nearly always been on the analysis of the work of art rather than on the process of the work's generation in the artist and the effects of this process upon the artist as a man.[44] But poets like Wordsworth and Coleridge and their continental counterparts evinced a degree of interest in and sensitivity toward the problems of creativity unknown before, and unknown most notably among their recent predecessors. Like other kinds of human progress, the process of poetry's becoming self-conscious tends to take place in spurts rather than continuously, and to take place at different rates in different places. Examination of the cause and effect relations involved in this intermittent pattern of development, with its variations according to locality, would fall properly within the field of cultural anthropology. But in any case, the development we are concerned with here was not an isolated phenomenon, limited to poetry and art.

There are a number of things which may have had a share in causing this development, or which at least point to some common causes. There was among people of various callings at the time a new tendency toward introspection, toward intimate self-examination, a specifically psychological as opposed to moral self-examination, a new interest in what Coleridge called "facts of

[43] *Situation of Poetry,* pp. 37-38.
[44] Abrams, in a passage already alluded to (p. 101), states as the intention of his book "to chronicle the evolution and (in the early nineteenth century) the triumph, in its diverse forms, of this radical shift to the artist in the alignment of aesthetic thinking. . . ."

mind," independent of though not yet often in total isolation from their moral significance.[45] Psychology as we know it today may be said to have had its birth in this period. People began to talk more often of the "mind" and less often of the "soul." This was surely in part a manifestation of that very general phenomenon, the rise of modern experimental science, the passion for accurate observation. From still another point of view, we may see a reaction against the immediate past, an insistence upon and fascination with detail as opposed to generalization, which the eighteenth century had performed so brilliantly, and often so carelessly, in its attempt to arrive at a final synthesis of all knowledge—a reaction against the Encyclopedia and the perfect aphorisms of Alexander Pope.

Parallel to this interest in detail as opposed to generalization in the realm of knowledge was the interest manifested in the individual as opposed to the class, the genus. Perhaps it can be said that the same factors which produced the great collectivizing forces that made themselves felt in the course of the nineteenth century (such things as industrialization, mass production, the dehumanization of nature, including human nature, by science, and such rationalizations thereof as Marxism) concurrently produced powerful forces in reaction to them, in defense of the integrity of the individual person and the specifically human.

Whatever the causes, whatever the complex of developments of which it was a part or aspect, the descent to a new level of reflective awareness of itself as a spiritual activity seems to be characteristic of Romantic poetry. One has only to count the number of poems written about poetry during the period to be convinced of it. And, in Maritain's words,

---

[45] T. S. Eliot is able to distinguish Baudelaire from his contemporaries by virtue of his perception of Evil, as opposed to Bad or Wrong (*Selected Essays*, New York: Harcourt, Brace, 1950), p. 380.

because man is a spirit *one* in substance with the flesh, in other words, a seriously incommoded spirit, this phenomenon takes place within him slowly and with difficulty, with extraordinary delays, and it involves errors.

And it is not accomplished without unhappy accidents.

As in each case in which thought attacks a different task, it begins, in the conquering of new domains, and especially the interior domains of its own spiritual universe, by bringing on troubles, disasters. The human being seems to disorganize itself, and it happens in fact sometimes that these crises of growth end badly. They are nevertheless crises of growth.[46]

Among English poets, Coleridge furnishes the clearest example of one of these crises.

Coleridge had given of himself, and of his most vital energies, to the poetic experience, asking of it at first, doubtless, no more than it is equipped to give; and nature, for its part, had responded by quickening in him the sources of creative power. The result was some great poetry, and some masterful analyses of the processes of its production. But from the very beginning there had been a tendency on his part to ask of this same experience something more, something categorically different, something which amounted to a direct mystical contact with God. Coleridge's nature was such that this kind of contact was acutely necessary to him. (We have seen how something similar happened to him in connection with the experience of human love, how he looked to it also for a kind of mystical fulfillment, and how he ended by destroying for himself the possibility of fruition in ordinary human love.)

We have at least one explicit statement from Coleridge which offers a description of his early poetic experience of nature, and in doing so expresses his recantation of the faith on which that ex-

[46] *Situation of Poetry*, p. 38.

perience was based. It is a marginal note made in Heinrich Steffens' *Anthropologie* (Breslau, 1822) opposite the following passage (I, 14-15):

But that feeling which plunges us into the fullness of Nature, that pure, holy feeling of spring which identifies us with the surging life of Nature in all its abundance, is the basis of anthropology. Whoever can hold fast to this feeling, the purest, the noblest, the most profound feeling of which man is capable, which never completely forsakes him and spreads a wonderful joy through his whole being, discovers at once that herein lies the source of his real freedom, which reveals as completely false the kind of pseudo-freedom he has tried to maintain by means of the discursive understanding, through selfish desire in foolish opposition to Nature, a freedom in which all fetters are broken, every wish fulfilled, all longing stilled, a freedom in which the blissfully expanded feeling transcends, in and with the ALL, the mutability of earthly existence.

"Thirty years ago," Coleridge says in his note,

in an Ode entitled France and in the last stanza ending with
     O Liberty! my spirit *felt* thee *there!*
I exprest the same thought: and as a Poet had a right to do so. But when this genial Flush is gone by, what answer has it left behind to the heart-withering Facts truly stated on p. 10?

Raysor notes that

Since Steffens discusses on p. 10 the facts of determinism, or Notwendigkeit, Coleridge is obviously making a recantation of some literary importance. He explicitly abjures the romantic naturalism of his youth.[47]

[47] T. M. Raysor, "Coleridge Marginalia," *Modern Language Notes*, XLIII (1928), 182. The original passage from Steffens follows:
"Aber jenes Gefühl, welches uns in der Fülle der Natur versenkt, jenes heilige, reine Frühlingsgefühl, welches das quellende Leben der Natur, als das eigene, uns gibt, und alle Reichthümer, als unsere, ist das Fundament der Anthropologie. Wer dieses Gefühl, das reinste, das herrlichste, das tiefste der Menschen, welches ihn nie ganz verlässt, welches eine wunderbare Freudigkeit über sein ganzes Daseyn verbreitet, festzuhalten vermag, der entdeckt unmittelbar, dass hier die

The passage from Steffens is an unusually good description of a full "natural" mystical experience, a *union* with nature, associated as it is with holiness, purity, involving the deepest experience of which man is capable and the direct, immediate discovery of ultimate freedom in identity with the absolute. Coleridge's poetic version is equally unequivocal: he feels himself "like a man beloved of God . . . pursuing fancies holy." He is inspired "beyond the guess of folly" (characteristically, the Englishman is on the defensive in such matters, where the Continental is not), and he experiences this same union ("And shot my being through earth, sea, and air, / Possessing all things with intensest love") in a spirit of "deep worship." There is no reason to suppose that the recantation Raysor speaks of was made at the time of the note (after 1822)—he had long since made that. The significance of the note for the present study lies in the clear evidence it offers of the definitely mystical character of Coleridge's early poetic experience.

Once he had become acutely aware of the remarkable virtualities of the authentic poetic experience of nature, it was perhaps his acute religious need, and the hope of having it fulfilled through poetic contact with nature, that led him toward pantheism. Or, on the contrary, perhaps other factors, in his make-up and deriving from his speculations, inclined him to pantheism in philosophy, and this inclination led him to place upon the poetic experience this too heavy burden. Conjecture on the order of causes in the matter is futile, but his deeply religious nature and his temporary estrangement from Christian faith were surely

---

Quellen seiner wahren Freiheit, der Punkt ist, wo jene Scheinfreiheit, die er durch den trennenden Verstand, durch die selbstsüchtigen Begierden im Gegensatz gegen die Natur thöricht behaupten möchte, völlig vernichtet wird, wo alle Ketten zerspringt, alle Wünsche erfüllt sind, alle Sehnsucht gestillt ist, in dem das selig, erweiterte Gefühl sich in und mit dem All über allen Wechsel des irdischen Daseyns erhaben fühlt."

relevant. In a letter written in 1816 he says that the complexity of his experience

> might have made of me a mere man of *observation,* if pain and sorrow and self-miscomplacence had not forced my mind in on itself, and so formed habits of meditation.[48]

Probably no man is *born* a *pèlerin de l'absolu:* he is born rather with the intellectual and spiritual capacity to become such, and it is the pains and sorrows of life which force him to realize that capacity. But the most noteworthy word here is "self-miscomplacence," surely a concocted word and therefore doubtless an effort to fix something quite accurately. With all of his personal circumstances taken duly into consideration as immediate causes, he is showing himself as moving in the deepest, most characteristic stream of romanticism. Speaking of Gérard de Nerval, Béguin says that

> Others as well have lived thus, in quest of some interior region, drawn from place to place by a gentle and nostalgic call, which only became painful from time to time, when it clarified itself and declared itself for what it was: the desire for salvation.[49]

Coleridge was led from poetry to love to abstruse researches, in *his* quest for salvation.

While he still had confidence in the efficacy of the poetic experience as "the way," he tended to overemphasize what Richards calls the "realist" view of the experience, to the point that the poet became an inanimate or very nearly inanimate harp across which the winds of the spirit of nature blew and made music—a self-prepared but merely passive receiver of the "influxes" of nature, i.e., of God's presence, nature *being* God, or, at the very least, a direct avenue to contact with him. Many years later,

---

[48] *Letters,* II, 659 (to James Gillman, April, 1816).
[49] *Gérard de Nerval,* p. 98.

Coleridge alluded to his period of pantheistic mysticism in declining to express an opinion concerning Bruno because he had read too little Bruno and that at a time when he was himself

intoxicated with the vernal fragrance and effluvia from the flowers and first-fruits of Pantheism, unaware of its bitter root, pacifying any religious feelings in the meantime by the fine distinction, that tho' God was=the World, the World was not=God—as if God were a whole composed of Parts of which the World was one![50]

At some point, doubtless when his need was most critical, he became aware, in however implicit terms, that, in the poetic transaction between nature and the poet, nature was not the immediately and personally active transmitter of the divine presence. In his actual experience of it, nature turned out *not* to be God. It became evident that the poetic experience of God was not the kind that produced the quietude of the mystic. In 1803 he wrote to his brother George:

I feel it more and more; all is vanity that does not lead to quietness and unity of heart, and to the silent awful idealess watching of that living spirit, and of that Life which passeth all understanding.[51]

The poetic experience itself had become vanity and, in the most excruciating way, vexation of spirit.

In his prospectus to *The Friend* Coleridge defines "dejection of mind" as "doubt or disbelief of the moral government of the world, and the grounds and arguments for the religious hopes of human nature."[52] Such a state of mind is no mere depression, and is not a state likely to be induced by inability to write poems, or by ill health and domestic difficulties. Having, by virtue of a

[50] Alice Snyder, "Coleridge on Giordano Bruno," *Modern Language Notes,* XLII (1927), 435. See also *Aids to Reflection* (1824) in *Complete Works,* I, 361-62, where he attacks the pantheism of "Tintern Abbey" and speaks of his own "brief period" of pantheism.
[51] *Unpublished Letters,* I, 285.
[52] *Complete Works,* II, 527.

new kind of reflexive awareness, isolated the poetic experience of nature from its normal fruition in a work *ad extra* and given himself up to it as one gives oneself up only to God, having sent his soul abroad expecting it to be received in the self-annihilating embrace of mystical union with the person of God, and having been disappointed, left in his own unbearable isolation,[53] Coleridge found himself in a literal incapacity to respond to nature.[54] He experienced what Béguin, citing Aragon, refers to as "ce grand échec qui se perpétue."

"It is strange," Béguin remarks,

if poetry and mysticism are indistinguishable, or even can be indistinguishable at some ideal stage never yet attained, that all poets have had the sensation of "that great *échec* which perpetuates itself," of which Aragon once spoke. In all times the poet has at certain moments had the impression of being damned, of being a "stealer of fire," a being exposed by his revolt to the divine wrath.[55]

And he cites the cases of Rimbaud, Racine, Baudelaire, and Nerval. But, asks Raïssa Maritain,

Such a feeling, quite different from a simple experience of the internal limitations of art, is it true that *all poets* necessarily experience it? It doubtless occurs the more frequently as the consciousness which poetry acquires of itself turns increasingly to the pure, unlimited desire for poetic knowledge, with which other hopes of the spirit come al-

---

[53] It is reported that "Coleridge . . . spoke of death with fear; not from the dread of punishment, not from the shrinking from physical pain, but he said he had a horror lest, after the attempt to 'shuffle off this mortal coil,' he should yet 'be thrown back upon himself' " (Sarah F. Adams, *Monthly Repository*, Vol. IX [1835]).

[54] Ten years later the inhibition still existed, and his description suggests its immediate psychological cause: "Sometimes when I earnestly look at a beautiful object or landscape, it seems as if I were on the *brink* of a fruition still denied— as if Vision were an *appetite;* even as a man would feel who, having put forth all his muscular strength in an act of prosilience, is at the very moment *held back* —he leaps and yet moves not from his place." *Anima Poetae*, p. 255 (among items from 1811-12).

[55] *Gérard de Nerval*, pp. 115-16.

most inevitably to be mixed. This feeling of disappointment, in any case, appears to be a distinctive characteristic of essential importance, and sufficient to show, even if it were the only thing, that poetry is not mysticism, and that the poet is preparing bitter disappointments for himself if he demands of Poetry that plenitude of spiritual knowledge which is found at the end of the ascetic and mystic ways. The mystics have never spoken of "that great *échec*." It is because they have experimental knowledge, more or less frequent, more or less profound, of that union with God which approaches perfect Unity. . . . Whatever otherwise are the trials of barrenness and denudation, the frightful nights that the soul traverses in the quest for union, even at the height of suffering it is never disappointed, provided it has to do with God and not with men. The plenitude of peace in the mystic, whether it be triumphant or subjacent to terrible combats, proves that he is not mistaken in proposing to attain Unity by the ways of sanctity. If poetry fulfilled our desires to this degree there would be no *"échec* that perpetuates itself"; nor would there be if one did not demand of poetry that it go up to the end of a way where, in any case, it cannot arrive alone. The error, here, witnesses moreover to the grandeur of Poetry, it is the proof of the kinship in the same divine source of the experience of the poet and that of the mystic. But all that poets and mystics have taught us about these things permits us to say, we believe . . . that if they draw from the same source, it is, however, with different dispositions, and according to essentially distinct types of relation to that Source.[56]

It is in terms like these that Coleridge's state at the moment he wrote "Dejection" can best be understood. He could no longer go out to nature. The poetic experience did not take place. And so, from the opposite extreme, from having attributed all the efficacy, all the life and passion of the poetic experience to a nature conceived as an immediate manifestation of the divine presence, he came to attribute all of the efficacy of the transaction to the poet, leaving nature a corpse.

Again we must look at the crucial lines from "Dejection":

[56] *Situation of Poetry*, pp. 32-33.

I may not hope from outward forms to win
The passion and the life, whose fountains are within.

IV

O Lady! we receive but what we give,
And in our life alone does Nature live:
Ours is her wedding garment, ours her shroud!
    And would we aught behold, of higher worth,
Than that inanimate cold world allowed
To the poor loveless ever-anxious crowd,
    Ah! from the soul itself must issue forth
A light, a glory, a fair luminous cloud
        Enveloping the Earth—
And from the soul itself must there be sent
    A sweet and potent voice, of its own birth,
Of all sweet sounds the life and element!

A good deal has been said about these lines as indications of a
decisive turn to Kantian idealism, but two things can be noted
immediately: that Coleridge is here quite obviously engaged in
analyzing the causes of the failure of his poetic powers, not in
pronouncing a philosophical doctrine, unless by implication; and
that, in the terms Maritain suggests (issuing from a realist philosophical position) there is nothing here which denies that "all
specification comes from the object."[57] Specification by the object
is neither absent—the poem is full of it—nor is the indispensa-
bility of its role denied. It is "the passion and the life, whose
fountains are within," which are in default, the "vital productivity," which comes "from the subjectivity itself."

As for the philosophical implication of the lines, they might as
well or better be interpreted as an approach to a realist scholastic
doctrine concerning the higher being things have in the mind.
According to this view, inanimate things achieve a more perfect
order of being when they exist as known to the senses, all sub-

[57] See in this book p. 157.

human things achieve a higher being when they exist as known by the intellect, and all things have their highest order of being in virtue of their existence in the mind of God, all of these being types of what the scholastics call "intentional being."[58] In this sense perhaps it *could* be said of nature that "ours is her wedding garment, ours her shroud!"

But in this view poetic knowledge, the kind of being things have in virtue of their new existence in the soul of the poet, is only possible because of correspondences (to use Baudelaire's word) or analogies (to use the scholastic term[59]) between the things known and the human knower, correspondences which depend ultimately on the fact that all are created by the one God. Involved here are the fundamental Thomist doctrines of the intelligibility of being and the analogy of being and the "transcendentals," Truth, Goodness, and Beauty. It would, as a matter of fact, be interesting, in tracing Coleridge's philosophical metamorphoses, to compare his "Ideas" and the "transcendentals" which for the scholastics form the basis of analogy.[60] By 1816, Coleridge acknowledged in a "Confessio Fidei," that

The wonderful works of God in the sensible world are a perpetual discourse, reminding me of His existence, and shadowing out to me His perfections. But as all language presupposes in the intelligent hearer or reader those primary notions, which it represents and excites us to combine,—even so I believe, that the notion of God is essential to the human mind; that it is called forth into distinct consciousness principally by the conscience, and auxiliarly by the manifest adaptation of means to ends in the outward creation.[61]

[58] See Maritain, quoted here p. 157, on the "superexistence of knowledge and the superexistence of love."

[59] On the subject of analogy, see, for instance, Anton van Leeuwen, "L'Analogie de l'Etre," *Revue Néoscholastique de Philosophie*, XXXIX (1936), 293-320.

[60] In a marginal note in Tenneman's *History of Philosophy*, Vol. VI, Coleridge speaks of "the Idea itself, the transcendental analogon of the Imagination or spiritual intuition" (quoted by Muirhead, *Coleridge as Philosopher*, p. 96).

[61] *Notes, Theological, Political, and Miscellaneous*, ed. by Derwent Coleridge

In any case, poetic *knowledge,* in this perspective, is not a creation at all, in the strict sense of the term, certainly not a creation
ex nihilo: it is an experience of the analogies of being, out of
which, certainly, a genuine if limited kind of creation may and
normally does issue through the process of artistic elaboration—
that "interminable building reared / By observation of affinities"
of which Wordsworth spoke. These analogies of being are, in
terms quite other than those employed in the laboratory, the
"secrets of the universe." It is no wonder that poets conceive fantastic ambitions for poetry, that they become enraptured, even to
the point of mistaking this knowledge of the Creator in and
through the signs of him left in his creation for an experience of
the person of God, or that, on discovering their error, they may
be inclined, as Coleridge was at the moment of "Dejection," to
deny any creative virtue to the world of nature.

In leaving nature a corpse, as he does in "Dejection," Coleridge
forces the poet to assume not only his proper role as a perceiver
of the analogies of being who embodies them in new objects, but
also the additional role of *creator* of those analogies. Formerly
nature was God, and it was necessary only to leave oneself passively open to its influxes. Now, in "Dejection," the poet must in
effect *be* God. Raïssa Maritain cites a passage from Moritz in
which he says that

since we could not, in order to equal God, become creators, we made
ourselves destroyers, we created backwards, since we could not create
in the direction of the future. We made for ourselves a universe of
destruction, and then, with a tender complacency, we contemplated
our work in history, in tragedy, and in our poems.[62]

(London: Ed. Moxon, 1853). See also *The Statesman's Manual* (1816), App. B,
p. 465.
   [62] *Situation of Poetry,* p. 28.

In England, this destructive reaction was left to a later generation of Romantics.

Mme Maritain remarks that "At the origin of such a deviation . . . there is the dazzlement of a real experience, in the heart of man, of that which surpasses man," and that this knowledge, if not "finally turned toward loving is by that very fact a source of death." Another deviation which has its origin in the same real experience, results from what may be called an opposite excess, not from a failure to turn the knowledge toward love but from expecting an order of response to one's love different from any that this experience is able to furnish. In this latter case as in the former, it turns out that through frustration the poet "wants to possess . . . [himself] of the chariot of God: to create for himself that interior enthusiasm which God alone can create."[63] At the moment of "Dejection" Coleridge is saying that the poet *must* possess himself of the chariot of God, that he *must,* in order to achieve the poetic experience, create for himself and as it were from scratch "that interior enthusiasm," because if it is nature he looks to for it he cannot find it. But he is at the same time recording his own inability to do this.

The new position, what Richards calls the "projective view," nevertheless embraces a truth absent from the former one—it is true that the poet is the source of the passion and the life; but these are awakened in him by the correspondences, the analogies, that he finds in nature. They are awakened in him by his poetic experience of the vitality of nature, not exuded from himself. If nature is a corpse to him, if it arouses no reverberations in his subjectivity, if, in other words, he is for whatever reason incapable of the poetic experience, then he is asking of himself the impos-

[63] *Ibid.,* pp. 28-29. This last quotation is attributed by Mme Maritain to C. H. von Schubert (1781-1860).

sible, though he "should gaze forever / On that green light that lingers in the west."

And it was not just poetry that Coleridge had lost, insofar as he had, but he had become aware that all the arts put together would not be sufficient to procure or express the consciousness for which he was striving, the knowing himself in God. Not long after the composition of "Dejection" he made the statement:

Without drawing I feel myself but half invested with language. Music too is wanting to me. But yet, though one should unite poetry, drafts-man's skill, and music, the greater and, perhaps, nobler, certainly *all* the subtler, parts of one's nature must be *solitary*. Man exists herein to himself and God alone—yes! in how much only to God! how much lies *below* his own consciousness![64]

Sounding the depths of nature and the depths of the self in the quest for the absolute, or for salvation, the poetic activity falls short of the goal. Béguin describes thus the whole tribe of Ro-mantics:

It is true that there is no escape from the torment of a cruel introspec-tion for these natures which bear in themselves the most intense mystical aspirations, without having the strength, or the grace, which would enable them to go up to the end of the mystical way. For such beings, subject to occasional ecstasies and to frequent relapses, the only possible progress is through becoming conscious of this internal predicament, which they sometimes feel as a blessing, and often resent as a heavy curse.[65]

The composition of "Dejection" was at least a step in Coleridge's *prise de conscience* of his internal misfortune: his intense mysti-cal aspirations, his lacking the force or the grace to go up to the end of the mystical way,[66] and his futile attempt to force the gates by means of love and the poetic experience.

[64] *Anima Poetae,* p. 31 (1802-03).
[65] *L'Ame Romantique,* I, 61-62.
[66] Or better, to adopt Mme Maritain's emendation of Béguin, his lacking the

If, as Béguin maintains, the poet at certain moments has the impression of being a condemned man, exposed to the wrath of God,[67] it is no doubt because at the root of his Promethean attempt there is a fundamental egoism. Having supposed nature to *be* God and the poetic experience therefore to be an immediate union with him, it is a short step from the discovery, more or less conscious, that nature is *not* God, to the attempt to *become* the God of nature, to become the Creator and Life-giver. Béguin says of Moritz:

He would always have to fight against this innate tendency of his personality, which he was later to call "egoism," and which consisted in considering the entire external world as a pure creation of the self.[68]

Certainly Coleridge was hovering on this brink in "Dejection," and it is at least as plausibly explicable in terms of the evolution of his poetic experience as in terms of an intellectual conversion to Kantianism, or a kind of pseudo-Kantianism.

Béguin records less definitive *échecs* in the cases of other Romantics—Novalis (1772-1801), Senancourt (1770-1846), Hölderlin (1770-1843). He quotes the following lines from Hölderlin's *Hyperion*:

> Ewig muss die liebste Liebe darben,
> Was wir lieben, ist ein Schatten nur,
> Da der Jugend goldne Träume starben,
> Starb für mich die freundliche Natur;
> Das erfuhrst du nicht in frohen Tagen,
> Dass so ferne dir die Heimat liegt,

---

grace to avoid confusing the poetic and mystic ways, and so expecting of the former what is only to be attained at the end of the latter.

[67] See in this book p. 177; and compare, for instance, the expressions of Rimbaud and Nerval, quoted here pp. 204-5.

[68] *L'Ame Romantique,* I, 64.

Armes Herz, du wirst sie nie erfragen,
Wenn dir nicht ein Traum von ihr genügt.[69]

So Coleridge, at the age of twenty-two, had no idea that the home-land lay so far away from him:

surely thou ere long shalt reach thy home,
And pleasant is the way that lies before.[70]

Thirty-three years later, at fifty-five, he does not know of love whether it was "real or a magic show,"[71] and makes himself content with a dream, seeing in the garden of Boccaccio:

in Dian's vest between the ranks
Of the trim vines, some maid that half believes
The vestal fires, of which her lover grieves,
With that sly satyr peeping through the leaves![72]

When we try to find close analogues to Coleridge's experience, we look in vain among his English contemporaries. Analogous expectations of poetry are numerous—one has only to think of Blake, of Wordsworth, or of Shelley—but it is necessary to go to the Continent to find cases in which this new deliberate exploration of the possibilities of poetic knowledge in and for itself had similarly destructive effects upon the explorers. In juxtaposing Coleridge's statements concerning mystical communion with nature and descent into the self with the statements of the German and French Romantics, no suggestion of "influence" is implied, although we know that Coleridge was familiar with the works of a number of them. In the first place, such tendencies are open

---

[69] *Ibid.*, II, 31-32. "Ever must the deepest love be famished; what we love is only a shadow. Once the golden dream of childhood faded, the friendliness of nature also died for me. In those happy days you did not know that the home-land lay so far away; poor heart, you shall never find it out, unless to dream of its suffices."

[70] *Poems*, p. 57.

[71] *Ibid.*, p. 468.

[72] *Ibid.*, p. 481.

to influence only in the vaguest way, if they are genuine, and not simply imitations of a kind of literary fad. And in the second place, anyone beginning to establish influence on Coleridge has to face the chastening effect of Coleridge's own warnings on the subject.[73] Rather, the effort is to make clearer what seems to be the true nature of these tendencies on Coleridge's part by juxtaposing them with more extreme examples of the same things.

The necessity that has so often been felt to "explain" Coleridge's personal, poetic, and philosophical difficulties by means of what are essentially extrinsic causes (opium, ill health, and so on), has been due in part to the fact that in the context of his compatriots he *does* appear something of a monster; whereas once placed in the company of the Continental Romantics, his case appears as a rather mild one. For reasons that would be of primary interest to a social anthropologist, we do not seem to find among English writers that complete lack of attention to being somehow respectable, that complete absence of the platform manner, that reckless concentration, which on the Continent produces genial monstrosities like Novalis or Rimbaud. The same difference may be felt in our own day, for instance, through the impression of strangeness that an English-speaking reader, especially if he has been nurtured on American literature and criticism, experiences on first reading a quantity of contemporary French literature— the sense of almost embarrassing if delicate intimacy, as if it were possible to write a book in the same tone of voice in which one speaks to one's friends. One gets the impression that French belles-lettres are really a kind of community correspondence among

---

[73] For instance, in reference to line 74 of "This Lime-Tree Bower," Coleridge appends the note: "Some months after I had written this line, it gave me pleasure to find that Bartram had observed the same circumstance of the Savanna Crane" (*Poems*, p. 181*n*). O Lowes, O Nethercott! And one recalls his much disputed defenses against plagiarism of German sources in connection with his philosophical writings.

French writers, published for convenience, and to collect a few francs from those interested in overhearing it.

But the difference between the English and the Continental mentality seems to exist also on a more fundamental level, of which this tone is only a symptom. In the Romantic period, the difference seems to have gone down to the level of the poetic-religious experience itself. One feels that an Englishman would have been somehow ashamed, embarrassed, even within the confines of his own soul, to give himself up to the spiritual "excesses" (and frequently abuses) of a Nerval or a Baudelaire (though Shelley can speak of "Staking his very life on some dark hope"). Insofar as he did, he was much more reserved in laying them bare to the public. And if this is true in some measure of English-speaking poets, the respectability of English-speaking critics and scholars constitutes a layer of almost impenetrable thickness insulating from view the spiritual conflicts and experiments of the poets they treat.

Although we have had occasion to note in passing a number of striking points of similarity between Coleridge's poetic experiences and those of various Continental Romantics, with the aim of seeing him in a European rather than exclusively British context, it would be interesting now to draw one comparison in greater detail, a comparison involving a difference not only of place but also of time. Of all continental *poètes maudits,* Rimbaud is most notorious, because his brief history was perhaps the most sensational of all, and because his relatively small opus had the most decisive effect in bringing what we think of as modern poetry to birth.[74] It is both surprising and instructive that he should offer a

[74] It should be noted that Rimbaud is also one of the most controversial of modern poets, authorities whom we may suppose to be equally respectable taking sharply contradictory views concerning him. An analysis of these controversies does not fall within the scope of the present study. The discussion which follows here will in effect, and quite unavoidably, reflect a single position rather than

Rimbaud born 18

relevant comparison with Coleridge: he was born twenty years after Coleridge's death (in Coleridge's detested France), and died at the age of thirty-seven after what may in every sense be called a violent life. But the fact is that there is a remarkable number of parallels between the two men. Both, for example, in the naïvete and inexperience of youth, attached themselves to violently revolutionary causes. Rimbaud was involved with the Communards, while Coleridge placed so genuine and enthusiastic a hope in the French Revolution that his disappointment therein colored his opinions for the rest of his life. Neither Coleridge nor Rimbaud was by nature or talents a political activist, and we may take these gestures as grasps at a kind of absolute, as expressions of an inchoate but quite basic dissatisfaction with things as they are: in youth it is possible to grasp at the absolute in concrete political terms. Both experiences resulted in prompt disillusion: the movements to which the two had attached themselves were quickly seen to betray the values they had, however obscurely, in mind. And both men made an effort on the same political level to start over from scratch on their own: Rimbaud composed a "Projet de Constitution Communiste," partially under the influence of Helvetius; Coleridge embarked upon the venture of Pantisocracy while he was under the influence of Hartley.

Although both of these men led what may be called very active lives, both of them evinced a basic distaste for action. A great deal has been said about Coleridge's laziness and indecisiveness, the paralysis of his will; but is it not possible that somewhere at the root of all this is the same will toward the absolute that drove both Coleridge and Rimbaud? Humphrey House calls at-

---

several divergent ones, a position derived from my own reading of him, influenced in an important degree by that of the Maritains. For other views, see, for instance, René Etiemble, *Le Mythe de Rimbaud* (Paris: Gallimard, 1952-54), and Carl A. Hackett, *Rimbaud* (London: Bowes & Bowes, 1957).

tention to Coleridge's disinclination to action, his attachment to
"facts of mind," and quotes a remark from a notebook that there
is "something inherently mean in action," that, as House puts it,
"the Almighty more or less made a mistake in creating the universe"[75] (and as a matter of fact theologians have some trouble
accounting for the fact that he did so). Rimbaud puts it in this
way:

I have a horror of all trades. Masters and workers—base peasants all.
The hand that guides the pen is worth the hand that guides the
plough.—What an age of hands! I shall never have my hand.[76]

And just so there is a sense in which Coleridge, although unlike
Rimbaud he went on writing to the day of his death instead of
vowing and keeping silence, *n'avait jamais sa main*. Rimbaud
comes even closer to what Coleridge seems to have been driving
at when he says that "I saw that all creatures have a fatality of
happiness: action is not life, but only a way of spoiling some
force, an enervation."[77] (Characteristically, the Frenchman goes
further, to the logical conclusion: "Morality is the weakness of
the brain.")

The contrary of "action" in this sense is, at the first remove,
contemplation, the simple being of other things through partici-
pating in their lives, as it were from inside, the most intense form
of the poetic experience of things:

It seemed to me that to every creature several *other* lives were due.
This gentleman knows not what he does: he is an angel. This family

[75] Coleridge says that "Even the creation of the universe disturbs my Idea of
the Almighty's greatness—would do so, but that I conceive that thought with
him creates" (House, *Coleridge,* pp. 13, 35).
[76] *A Season in Hell,* p. 7. In the original French, the third sentence reads: "La
main à plume vaut la main à charrue." It seems to me that the verb "vaut" here
may better be taken in the sense which it has in the expression "L'un vaut
l'autre": one is as good, or as bad, as the other; there is nothing to choose between them. Understood in this way, Rimbaud is saying something like "The
hand that guides the pen is worth *no* more *than* the hand that guides the plough."
[77] *Ibid.,* p. 65.

is a litter of puppies. With several men I have spoken with a moment of one of their lives. Thus it was that I loved a pig.[78]

One is immediately reminded of Coleridge's early poem "To a Young Ass" (1794),[79] in which he hails the animal *"Brother—spite of the fool's scorn,"* and which Warren singles out as an early example of the theme of "sacramental vision," along with "Religious Musings" and "The Eolian Harp."[80]

But the ultimate, the archetype of this contrary of action in the human sense, is what theologians call the self-contemplation of God, which includes a knowledge of all things in their most intimate being, as they can only be known by one who has created them *ex nihilo,* by one whose every work is a perfect word. This is a knowledge which, according to orthodox theology, is to be shared by the human soul when it comes to share the life of God in the beatific vision and which will constitute infinite happiness. The theologians also maintain that the longing for this estate, however obscure and implicit, is somehow at the root of all human longings and ambitions, and is the source both of joys and of torments: it is in this perspective that we may understand Rimbaud's otherwise cryptic statement that all beings "have a fatality of happiness" and Coleridge's agonizing over the loss of joy, of which he says:

In joy individuality is lost and it therefore is liveliest in youth, not from any principle of organization but simply from this that the hardships of life, that the circumstances that have forced a man in upon his little unthinking contemptible self, have lessened his power of existing universally; it is that only which brings about those passions. To have genius is to live in the universal, to know no self but that which is reflected not only from the faces of all around us, or fellow creatures, but reflected from the flowers, the trees, the beasts,

---

[78] *Ibid.*
[79] *Poems,* pp. 76-78.
[80] "A Poem of Pure Imagination," p. 127 (n. 63).

yea from the very surface of the waters and the sands of the desert. A man of genius finds a reflex to himself, were it only in the mystery of being.[81]

And this joy is just the contrary of action, in which "the overbusy worldlings are buzzed around by night-flies in a sultry climate."[82]

Rimbaud records his attempts to achieve this absolute in words that remind us of Coleridge at many points, though Rimbaud's was doubtless an even more desperately ambitious quest. After recording his loving a pig, Rimbaud goes on:

Not a single sophistry of madness—madness to be confined—was forgotten: I could recite them all again, I know the system.

My health was threatened. Terror came. I would fall into a slumber of days, and getting up would go on with the same sad dreams. I was ripe for death and along a road of perils my weakness led me to the confines of the world and of Cimmeria, home of whirlwinds and of darkness.[83]

All this because of

Happiness! Its tooth deadly sweet, warned me at the crowing of the cock,—*ad matutinem,* at the *Christus venit,*—in the darkest cities:

And there follows a poem which in a totally non-discursive fashion is reminiscent of "Dejection":

> O saisons, ô châteaux!
> Quelle âme est sans défauts?
>
> J'ai fait la magique étude
> Du bonheur, qu'aucun n'élude.
>
> Salut à lui chaque fois
> Que chante le coq gaulois
>
> Ah! je n'aurai plus d'envie:
> Il s'est chargé de ma vie.

---

[81] *Philosophical Lectures,* p. 179.
[82] *Ibid.,* p. 168.
[83] *A Season in Hell,* p. 65.

> Ce charme a pris âme et corps
> Et dispersé les efforts.

> O saisons, ô châteaux!

> L'heure de la fuite, hélas!
> Sera l'heure du trépas.

> O saisons, ô châteaux![84]

And so we have what is conventionally called laziness presented as the highest kind of superactivity. As Coleridge says, "there is something inherently mean in action":

> Ce charme a pris âme et corps
> Et dispersé les efforts.

The paradox is rich, and an outrage to the industrious bystander. Coleridge might almost have written:

As for established happiness, domestic or not . . . no, I cannot. I am too dissipated, too weak. Life flourishing through toil, old platitude! As for me, my life is not heavy enough, it flies and floats far above action, that precious focus of the world.[85]

---

[84] *Oeuvres de Arthur Rimbaud* (Paris: Mercure de France, 1947), pp. 224-25. Miss Varese gives the following translation of these lines (p. 67):

> O seasons, O castles!
> What soul is without sin!

> The magic study I've made
> Of happiness none can evade.

> To it each time, good luck,
> We hear the Gallic cock.

> No more desires for me:
> It has taken my life in fee.

> Charmed body, soul and brain
> Delivered of every strain.

> O seasons, O castles!

> The hour of flight will be
> The hour of death for me!

> O seasons, O castles!

[85] *A Season in Hell*, p. 23.

Coleridge certainly could be said to have taken off and floated above action—the Southeys and Wordsworths were by turns pitying and furious, his wife was doubtless consistently furious. Unfortunately, Coleridge did not realize clearly at nineteen as did Rimbaud that "established happiness, domestic or not" was not for him. But it was this ambition, this supernal "laziness," which led both Rimbaud and Coleridge to ask the impossible of poetry. "Dejection," like *Une Saison en Enfer,* records "L'heure de la fuite," and in both cases it was "l'heure du trépas." Rimbaud was left crying out, in a kind of desperate nostalgia, "O saisons, ô châteaux!" Coleridge gazing listlessly on "that green light in the west," like

> a little child
> Upon a lonesome wild,
> Not far from home, but she hath lost her way.

Their original ambition for poetry shows itself first in their common reaction to the poetry of their predecessors, which is at bottom not an objection to false style but to a conception of the nature and role of poetry which they felt that style evinced. Rimbaud goes further than Coleridge in dismissing the past, perhaps because he had no Shakespeare to look back upon:

> From Greece to the Romantic movement—the middle ages—we find men of letters, versifiers. From Ennius to Theroldus, from Theroldus to Casimir Delavigne, it's all rimed prose.[86]

In Coleridge's words, "thoughts *translated* into the language of poetry." In using these words Coleridge was not only calling attention to the necessity for what Warren calls symbolic extension as opposed to direct transcription,[87] but also scoring a kind of

---

[86] *La Lettre du Voyant,* in *Un Coeur sous un Soutane, Précédé de La Lettre du Voyant* (Paris: Presses du Livre Français, 1950), p. 22. All passages quoted from this work are my own translations.

[87] See in this book p. 152.

"poetry" based on no poetic experience as he had come to understand that experience, and, more fundamentally still, based on a
conception of the universe and man's relation to it which he had
come to consider as false and even viciously superficial. He makes
the point very clearly in the *Biographia Literaria* in commenting
on Wordsworth's criticism of a sonnet by Gray:

That the 'Phoebus' is hackneyed, and a schoolboy image, is an *accidental* fault, dependent on the age in which the author wrote, and not
deduced from the nature of the thing. That it is part of an exploded
mythology, is an objection more deeply grounded. Yet when the torch
of ancient learning was re-kindled, so cheering were its beams, that
our eldest poets, cut off by Christianity from all *accredited* machinery,
and deprived of all *acknowledged* guardians and symbols of the great
objects of nature, were naturally induced to adopt, as a *poetic* language, those fabulous personages, those forms of the* supernatural in
nature, which had given them such dear delight in the poems of their
great masters. Nay, even at this day what scholar of genial taste will
not so far sympathize with them, as to read with pleasure in PETRARCH,
CHAUCER, or SPENSER, what he would perhaps condemn as puerile in
a modern poet?

   * But still more by the mechanical school of philosophy which has
needlessly infected our theological opinions, and teaching us to consider the world in its relation to God, as of a building to its mason,
leaves the idea of omnipresence a mere abstract notion in the stateroom
of our reason.[88]

It is in terms like these that we must understand the ultimate reaction of men like Coleridge and Rimbaud to their predecessors.
Again, Rimbaud is more violent:

   Musset is execrable to the fourteenth degree for us, mournful gen-
erations caught up by visions, whom his angelic sloth has insulted!
Oh *Nuits!* Oh Rolla, oh Namouna, oh la Coupe! It's all French, another way of saying supremely detestable, French, not Parisian. Still

[88] II, 58-59.

another product of that abominable genius that inspired Rabelais, Voltaire, Jean de la Fontaine, annotated by M. Taine![89]

How enthusiastically Coleridge would have concurred in the judgment "Tout est français, c'est-à-dire haïssable au suprème degré," without feeling Rimbaud's necessity to add the qualification, "français, pas parisien." And this suggests a fundamental and more plausible basis for Coleridge's seemingly inordinate distaste for all things French than resentment at having been taken in by the French Revolution, or a kind of Anglo-Saxon puritanism: it seems safe to say that just as the French Romantics carried the romantic ideal further into action than their fellows across the Channel, so the French Neo-classicists represented a kind of ultimate extreme. Rolland de Renéville explains the matter thus:

The 17th and 18th centuries were really dazzled by the harmony of Greek art without grasping the factors which gave rise to it. Taking the word *reason* as a synonym for *good sense* resulted in the elevation of a certain mediocrity of mind to the status of a dogma. There was no other cause for the flowering of the hideous French genius. If there existed certain great souls, it was only insofar as they shook off the yoke to which they thought they were submitting. The first Romantics endeavored to free themselves from these conventions and to rediscover their soul, but we must await the generation that followed them to see some results of this effort.[90]

As we know, Coleridge spent the better part of his mature life belaboring the distinction between Reason and Understanding, and for him as for Rimbaud the French Neo-classicists were the great champions of the Understanding.

This reaction of both men to neo-classical convention of thought as well as style took many forms. One thinks, for instance, of

[89] *Lettre du Voyant,* p. 31.
[90] *Rimbaud le Voyant* (Paris: Au Sans Pareil, 1929), p. 20.

Coleridge's fascination with the neo-Platonists and the Christian mystics, who, he said, served to keep the heart alive in the head, and of Rimbaud's preoccupation with oriental mysticism, which he discusses in a section of *Une Saison en Enfer* called "L'Impossible":

Having recovered two cents worth of reason,—it is soon gone!—I see that my disquietudes come from having understood too late that we are in the Occident.

Like Coleridge, he had supposed himself to be, or acted as if he were, in Xanadu. "The occidental swamps!" he continues:

Not that I think light faded, form shrunk, movement lost . . . Well! here is my spirit insisting on taking upon itself all the cruel developments that the spirit has suffered since the end of the Orient . . . It really insists, my spirit!

. . . My two cents worth of reason is spent! Spirit is in command, it insists that I be in the Occident. I'd have to silence it to conclude as I wished.

To the devil, I said, with the martyrs' crowns, the beams of art, the pride of inventors, the ardor of plunderers; I returned to the Orient and to the first and eternal wisdom. —A dream of vulgar indolence, it would seem![91]

Coleridge was never quite able, like Rimbaud in this passage, to say to hell with the Christian tradition, with the heritage of art, with the discoveries of science, or even with the urge to imperialism. He was, after all, and in some ways before all, an Englishman. But for both men Poetry, the poetic experience, offered the primary "way," and it was a desolating thing to be called back to the Occident, to a world in which "all *things* appear *little*."

Poets have always had a tendency to make exalted claims con-

---

[91] *A Season in Hell*, p. 71. It may be true as Enid Starkie suggests (*Arthur Rimbaud*, New York, W. W. Norton, 1947, p. 100), that Rimbaud's knowledge of Eastern thought was superficial and derived largely from secondary sources, but his preoccupation with it is no less significant for that fact.

cerning the nature and role of poetry, claims which strike the layman as more or less exaggerated. Even the layman who appreci-
ates poetry as the embodiment of the most cherished human
perceptions of value is likely to be somewhat skeptical of claims
which seem to lift poetry out of the realm of art, of something to
be contemplated and loved in and for itself but which is *practically*
useless, and to attribute to it some kind of super-utility. When
Coleridge says he hopes to achieve a poetry which will "supersede all metaphysics and morals,"[92] when Rimbaud says that the
poet must *"be a seer,* make himself a *seer,"* that he becomes "the
supreme Savant,"[93] one is inclined to interpret such statements as
metaphors, as ways of saying simply that poetry is very, very important, and one may be inclined to agree on that basis.

But in fact such statements are not metaphorical at all. Once
the poet becomes explicitly conscious of poetic knowledge of the
world as a distinct kind of knowledge, the possibilities seem limit-
less. He has become conscious of the analogies of being, and of
the possibility of perceiving them through a knowledge by connaturality, of knowing things by *experiencing* them, by partici-
pating immediately in their very being in virtue of the correspondences existing between their being and his own—instead of
knowing them piecemeal and from afar, as is the way of reason
and discursive knowledge. It is as if suddenly one discovered it
possible to learn about people by reading their minds instead of
having to ask them questions, or better yet, as if one could learn
about them by reading one's *own* mind.

And it will not do to dismiss such claims as fanciful nonsense,
for there is so much truth in them. Poetic knowledge, like other
kinds of knowledge by connaturality, *is,* by its very nature, more
intimate, more deeply possessed, and more universally extensible

[92] *Letters,* I, 347 (to Humphrey Davy, February, 1801).
[93] *Lettre du Voyant,* pp. 24-25.

than discursive, or scientific, knowledge.[94] The scholastics would say that it is an approximation to the immediate knowledge supposed to be possessed by unembodied spirits, by the angels,[95] the nearest approximation possible to spirits encumbered with a body. "So," Maritain remarks, "the spiritual virtue of human art, once it has attained a certain altitude in its own heaven, perceives itself to be translating by analogies and symbols the movement of a superior, unattainable sphere."[96] And so it is that Rimbaud declares the poet to be "vraiment un voleur de feu."[97] Rolland de Renéville gives an admirable summary of Rimbaud's metaphysical and scientific ambition for poetry:

> The universe is an act of sensual pleasure. Things are formed by the union of contrary atoms which, in joining, constitute the matter of the world. The most dissimilar realities entwine their secret branches.
>
> The function of the poet is to reveal the unity of the world. He must achieve this by means of images, that is, by disclosing the close correspondences which exist between apparently distinct realities. The more considerable their difference, the more the poet's images will reveal of universal unity.
>
> In the first fire of this discovery Rimbaud composed the SONNET OF VOWELS, in which he shows the remarkable relations between sounds and colors, and presents a manifestation of the law of unity.[98]

As Coleridge puts it, "True philosophy is comprised in the study of the science and language of symbols." But the whole passage, from *The Statesman's Manual,* deserves note:

---

[94] A most subtle and illuminating treatment of this whole subject of the "degrees of knowledge" is to be found in Jacques Maritain's *Distinguer pour Unir, ou les Degrés du Savoir* (Paris: Alcan, 1932), newly translated under the supervision of Gerald P. Phelan as *Distinguish to Unite; or, The Degrees of Knowledge* (New York: Scribner's, 1959).

[95] See in this book pp. 54-55.

[96] *Art and Scholasticism,* p. 78.

[97] *Lettre du Voyant,* p. 28.

[98] *Rimbaud le Voyant,* p. 26.

That which we find in ourselves is *(gradu mutato)* the substance and the life of all our knowledge. Without this latent presence of the 'I am,' all modes of existence in the external world flit before us as colored shadows, with no greater depth, root, or fixture, than the image of a rock hath in a gliding stream or the rainbow on a fast-sailing rain-storm. The human mind is the compass, in which the laws and actuations of all outward essences are revealed as the dips and declinations. . . . The power delegated to nature is all in every part: and by a symbol I mean, not a metaphor or allegory or any other figure of speech or form of fancy, but an actual and essential part of that, the whole of which it represents. Thus our Lord speaks symbolically when he says that *the eye is the light of the body.* The genuine naturalist is dramatic poet in his own line: and such as our myriad-minded Shakespeare is, compared with the Racines and Metastasios, such and by a similar process of self-transformation would the man be, compared with the doctors of the mechanic school, who should construct his physiology on the heaven-descended, Know Thyself.[99]

Coleridge again and again enunciates this essential identity of science and poetry, based upon connatural knowledge of the analogies of being. In *The Friend* he says that the "substances" of the chemistry laboratory

are symbols of elementary powers, and the exponents of a law, which, as the root of all these powers, the chemical philosopher, whatever his theory may be, is instinctively laboring to abstract. This instinct, again, is itself but the form, in which the idea, the mental correlative of the law, first announces its incipient germination in his own mind. . . . This is, in truth, the first charm of chemistry, and the secret of the almost universal interest excited by its discoveries. The serious complacency which is afforded by the sense of truth, utility, performance, and progression, blends with and ennobles the exhilarating surprise and the pleasurable sting of curiosity, which accompany the propounding and the solving of an enigma. It is the sense of a principle of connection given by the mind, and sanctioned by the cor-

[99] p. 465.

Pietro Trapassi 1698-1782
- improvisatore. Libretto-writer,
singer, musician

respondency of nature. Hence the strong hold which in all ages chemistry has had on the imagination. If in Shakespear we find nature idealized into poetry, through the creative power of a profound yet observant meditation, so through the meditative observation of a Davy, a Wollaston, or a Hatchett:

> By some connatural force,
> Powerful at greatest distance to unite
> With secret amity things of like kind,

we find poetry, as it were, substantiated and realized in nature,—yea, nature itself disclosed to us, *geminam istam naturam, quae fit et facit, et creat et creatur,* as at once poet and the poem.[100]

This might be taken as a reflection of the transcendentalism or Kantian idealism so often attributed to Coleridge, if not to Rimbaud, but that in the passages here under consideration both of them seem rather to be manifesting a new grasp of a much older, a virtually perennial doctrine, and making a new use of it. When Coleridge says that

In Man the centripetal and individualizing tendency of all Nature is itself concentred and individualized—he is a revelation of Nature! Henceforward, he is referred to himself, delivered up to his own charge; and he who stands the most on himself, and stands the firmest, is the truest, because the most individual, Man. In social and political life this acme is interdependence; in moral life it is independence; in intellectual life it is genius. Nor does the form of polarity, which has accompanied the law of individuation up its whole ascent, desert it here. As the height, so the depth. The intensities must be at once opposite and equal. As the liberty, so must be the reverence for law. As the independence, so must be the service and the submission to the Supreme Will! As the ideal genius and the originality, in the same proportion must be the resignation to the real world, the sympathy and the intercommunion with Nature. In the conciliating midpoint, or equator, does the Man live, and only by its poles can that life be manifested![101]

[100] pp. 427-28.
[101] *Theory of Life,* included as Appendix C to *Aids to Reflection,* in *Works,* ed. by Shedd, I, 412.

he is much closer to St. Thomas than to Kant, and to a tradition much older than St. Thomas. As Etienne Gilson explains concerning St. Thomas:

In conformity with Dionysius' principle that what is highest in the inferior order touches the lower confines of the superior order, St. Thomas puts man between angel and animal, reaching up to the former at the summit of his intellectual powers, and down to the latter in respect of his perishable body. It is in this very precise sense that man is a 'microcosm,' a whole universe in little, 'for in him everything else in the world is, in some way, represented.' That, moreover, is why St. Thomas adds that the soul is a kind of frontier or horizon between two worlds, the meeting place of pure spirits and irrational animals. Thus Christian philosophy extends in a two-fold direction the field to be explored by man in the study of himself: the moralists oblige him to examine conscience for the sake of progress in the interior life, the philosophers reintroduce a certain measure of that physicism which the moralist tends to ignore. The miniature world of man will never be known unless we know something of the greater. Hence the repeated efforts made by the men of the Middle Ages, and even by those of the Renaissance, to evolve complete anthropologies, in which a detailed description of the body leads to that of the soul, and this in its turn to the knowledge of God.[102]

On the basis of a similar faith in the unity of the world and man's strategic place in it, poets like Coleridge and Rimbaud proposed to themselves a poetic knowledge which would be truly universal. If it is important to try to understand wherein their quest for a complete anthropology based on poetic knowledge was finally as futile as the Medieval quest for a complete anthropology based on rational deduction, it is equally important to place their quest in a sufficiently long perspective to see how it represents a genuine evolution, a genuinely new attack upon a perennial human problem, an attack which had never before been in the same

[102] *The Spirit of Medieval Philosophy,* translated by A. H. C. Downes (New York: Scribners, 1936), pp. 218-19.

way possible, and which, although it failed to attain its envisaged goal, extended the frontiers of human consciousness.

In the same way that poetry was to take the place of metaphysics, it was also to take the place of morals. In Rimbaud's words, the poet "is responsible for mankind, for the animals even; he must make his inventions felt, touched, heard; . . ."[103] "Art as an enduring force," he says, "has its functions, since poets are citizens. Poetry will not simply put rhythm into action; it will be *ahead of it.*"[104] For Coleridge, the great model of poetry as action was Martin Luther. The particular action he singled out was Luther's throwing the inkpot at the devil, and it is a good illustration of what Rimbaud means by saying that poetry "sera *en avant.*" Coleridge brings up the inkpot incident in the process of likening Luther and Rousseau as men whose distinguishing characteristic was their "sensibility." He presents Luther not as a great theologian, or as a great moralist, not, in short, as a great discursive thinker, but as one who attained moral truth through what were really exercises of poetic sensibility:

He deemed himself gifted with supernatural influxes, an especial servant of heaven, a chosen warrior fighting as the general of a small but faithful troop, against an army of evil beings, headed by the prince of the air. These were no metaphorical beings, in his apprehension. He was a poet indeed, as great a poet as ever lived in any age or country; but his poetic images were so vivid, that they mastered the poet's own mind! He was possessed with them, as with substances distinct from himself: Luther did not write, he acted poems.[105]

Note that it is *Coleridge* who identifies Luther's actions as arising from a poetic source. He clearly does not believe, as Luther presumably did, that the devil really appeared to him, that the ex-

---

[103] *Lettre du Voyant*, p. 28.
[104] *Ibid.*, p. 29.
[105] *The Friend*, p. 131.

perience, or others like it, was the result of a specifically supernatural "influx." But Coleridge just as clearly *does* believe that what he characterizes as Luther's poetic way of determining action, Luther's poetic morality, is superior to the purely rational way (he had long ago stated that "all truth is a species of revelation").[106]

One might defend Luther by disagreeing with Coleridge, by maintaining that his inspiration was authentically supernatural and *therefore* superseded reason; but if one accepts Coleridge's account, it offers itself more readily as an explanation of what might be considered deplorable in the ultimate character of Luther's actions, and one might proceed to say of Luther, as Maritain says of Rimbaud, that his

error consists in . . . forcibly transferring poetry from the line of art to the line of morality, . . . now poetry is being made the means of life (and death).

What Maritain goes on to say would, in the perspective of one who considered Luther to be fundamentally in error, be specifically applicable to Luther—if one accepted Coleridge's analysis.

As for the sphere of action and human destiny, what element can poetry as regulating moral and spiritual life, poetry to *be realized in action,* introduce that is not counterfeit? Counterfeit of the supernatural and the miraculous, of grace and the heroic virtues. Disguised as an angel of counsel, it will lead the human soul astray on false mystic ways; and its spirituality, perverted from its meaning and diverted from its true place, under the appearance of a wholly profane interior conflict will give a new development to the old heresies of the free spirit.[107]

Maritain would probably be inclined to accept Coleridge's analysis of the springs of Luther's actions, and to consider this as at

[106] *Letters,* I, 352 (to Thomas Poole, March 23, 1801).
[107] *Art and Scholasticism,* p. 80.

least a partial explanation for what he considered to be the error of Luther's ways, which he surely believes to involve the "old heresies of the free spirit." The point here, however, is that although Coleridge did not go so far as either Luther, Rousseau, or Rimbaud in implementing the substitution of poetry for morals, he was in the same line.

Coleridge and Rimbaud agree further in their emphasis on the element of introspection in the poetic experience. Because it is based upon the connaturality subsisting between the human soul and the universe outside, or Nature, this poetic superknowledge which is to supersede all metaphysics and morals can be attained almost indiscriminately through the study of nature or the study of the self. Given this principle, the contradiction is only apparent between the Romantics' insistence upon passive openness to the influxes of nature, "wisely forgetful" of self, and their equal insistence upon what Coleridge so many times refers to as "the heaven-descended Know Thyself." Rimbaud puts it in this way:

The first study of a man who wants to be a poet is his own consciousness, in its entirety; he searches in his soul, inspects it, tries it, learns it. Once he knows it, he must cultivate it! That seems easy: in every brain a natural development takes place; so many *egoists* proclaim themselves authors; there are plenty of others who attribute to themselves their intellectual progress! But it's a question of making the soul monstrous: in the manner of the *comprachicos,* why not? Imagine a man planting and cultivating warts on his face.[108]

This goes a good deal further than what is ordinarily understood by the classic maxim, Know thyself. If one is to find all knowledge within the soul, really and immediately, then the soul's most secret virtualities must be "cultivated." One is reminded of the "experiments" that Coleridge was performing at Keswick in 1801, experiments involving the senses, which left him utterly exhausted

[108] *Lettre du Voyant,* p. 24.

and contributed to his illness and, doubtless, to his indulgence in laudanum.[109] One gets the general impression that Coleridge's cultivation of his soul, of the marvels and especially of the monstrosities hidden within it, was less deliberate than that described by Rimbaud. He was perhaps not one to plant and cultivate warts on his face, but if they grew there he certainly inspected them with something like the same metaphysical curiosity, and as we know, they were, figuratively speaking, many. The poet makes himself a seer, says Rimbaud,

by a long, immense, and reasoned *derangement* of *all the senses*. All the forms of love, of suffering, of madness; he searches himself, he drains off all the poisons in him, to keep only their quintessences.

And he describes the results to the human person thus:

Ineffable torture, in which he needs all the faith, all the superhuman strength [of which he is capable], in which he becomes beyond all others the critical case, the great criminal, the great outcast—and the supreme Savant!—For he arrives at the *unknown*. Because he has cultivated his soul, already rich, richer than any other! He arrives at the unknown and when, panic-stricken, he might end up losing his understanding of his visions, he has *seen* them. Let him perish in bounding through unheard-of and un-nameable things: there will come other horrible laborers; they will begin at the horizons where the other collapsed.[110]

It was at least in part such "ineffable torture" as this which "rendered any subjects immediately concerned with feeling, a source of pain and disquiet" to Coleridge,[111] and which explains his flight from poetry.

---

[109] *Letters,* I, 348-49 (to Thomas Poole, March 16, 1801).

[110] *Lettre du Voyant,* pp. 24-25.

[111] See in this book p. 14. Béguin quotes Gérard de Nerval in a similar vein: "Perhaps I was damned for having wanted to penetrate a deadly mystery in contradiction to divine law; henceforth I could only expect anger and contempt!" (*Gérard de Nerval,* p. 38).

But the refuge of metaphysics was illusory or at best temporary, for the same process was at work therein. As early as 1794 Coleridge told Southey that he was

> so habituated to philosophizing that I cannot divest myself of it, even when my own wretchedness is the subject. I appear to myself like a sick physician, feeling the pang acutely, yet deriving a wonted pleasure from examining its progress and developing its causes.[112]

And in a notebook entry appearing in the *Anima Poetae* with items from 1802 he says that

> Metaphysics make all one's thoughts equally corrosive on the body, by inducing a habit of making momently and common thought the subject of uncommon interest and intellectual energy.[113]

Rimbaud would have understood very well the kind of exercise Coleridge describes in another notebook entry:

> Hung over the Bridge, & musing considering how much of this Scene of endless variety in Identity was Nature's—how much the living organ's! What would it be if I had the eyes of a fly! —What if the blunt eye of a Brobdignag!—[114]

All this study of the soul, all these exercises, including the "déréglement des sens," was to issue in a universal language, another great Romantic dream. Coleridge hoped to be able

> to evolve all the five senses, that is, to deduce them, from one sense, and to state their growth and the causes of their difference, and in this evolvement to solve the process of life and consciousness. *I write this to you only, and I pray you, mention what I have written to no one.* At Wordsworth's advice, or rather fervent entreaty, I have intermitted the pursuit.[115]

---

[112] *Letters,* I, 106-7 (December 11, 1794).
[113] p. 23.
[114] Notebook No. 21. Add. MSS 47518, f. 56, quoted by House, *Coleridge,* p. 56.
[115] *Letters,* I, 348-49 (to Thos. Poole, March 16, 1801).

He was concerned with

the necessity of reconciling the restlessness of an ever-working Fancy with an intense craving after a resting-place for my Thoughts in some *principle* that was derived from experience, but of which all other knowledge should be but so many repetitions under various limitations, even as circles, squares, triangles, etc., etc., are but so many positions of spaces.[116]

Rimbaud puts it in these terms:

To find a language; moreover every word being an idea, the time of a universal language will come!

This language will be from soul to soul, embodying everything— odors, sounds, colors—thought catching onto thought and pulling.[117]

One result in Rimbaud's case was the famous "Sonnet des Voy- *see* p. 198 elles," in which the attempt is made to arrive at a definitive symbolism of colors. Long before Rimbaud, Coleridge had suggested that

A far more subtle and difficult, yet I would fain believe not hopeless investigation than an analysis of line would be respecting the symbolical characters or Significancy of Colors. But for this I am not prepared—I can merely glimpse it from the Mount Pisgah in the distance.[118]

He was interested in the fact that "A dunghill at a distance sometimes smells like musk, & a dead dog like elder-flowers—"[119] It is in lines added to "The Eolian Harp" as late as 1817 that we find the most famous and most significant expression of the universal language idea, based upon experience of the correspondences of nature:

---

[116] Quoted by Coburn, *Inquiring Spirit*, pp. 33-34.
[117] *Lettre du Voyant*, pp. 28-29.
[118] Coburn, *Inquiring Spirit*, pp. 215-16.
[119] *Notebooks*, ed. by Coburn, Vol. I, entry 223 G. 219.

> O! the one Life within us and abroad
> Which meets all motion and becomes its soul,
> A light in sound, a sound-like power in light,
> Rhythm in all thought, and joyance everywhere.[120]

Nature is a great poem, and the poet hardly knows whether he is the poet or the poem—*geminam istam naturam, quae fit et facit, et creat et creatur.*[121]

If for any reason the poet comes to feel responsible for the correspondences, then poetry, the germination of poetic symbols, becomes *absolute* creation, what Rimbaud calls "l'Alchimie du Verbe." This is the kind of poetic creation Coleridge was implicitly asking of himself in "Dejection." Or, on the other hand, in the manner of Coleridge's early poems like "The Eolian Harp," the poet feels himself pure instrument. In either case, the *poem,* the artistic elaboration of the poetic experience, tends to become incidental. As Rimbaud says,

Romanticism has never been properly judged. Who would have judged it? The Critics!! The Romantics? who prove so thoroughly that the song so infrequently constitutes the work, that is to say the very thought, sung and understood by the singer.

For *I* is an other. If the wind-instrument turns out to be a bugle, it's not its fault. This much is obvious to me: I am a witness of the birth of my thought: I watch it, I listen to it: I make a stroke with the bow: the symphony stirs in the depths, or leaps with a single bound to the surface.[122]

Coleridge in this particular connection had gone even further than Rimbaud was to go—with the eolian harp no "stroke of the bow" is necessary:

---

[120] *Poems,* p. 101, and note. Meyer Abrams may not be fully justified in the case of Coleridge in saying that inter-sensory images were employed by the English poets only casually, "without a specific rationale in aesthetic theory" (*The Mirror and the Lamp,* p. 94).

[121] Béguin quotes Victor Hugo as asking himself in 1834, "up to what point the singing belongs to the voice, and the poetry to the poet?" (*Gérard de Nerval,* p. 126).

[122] *Lettre du Voyant,* pp. 22-23.

> And what if all of animated nature
> Be but organic Harps diversely fram'd,
> That tremble into thought, as o'er them sweeps
> Plastic and vast, one intellectual breeze,
> At once the Soul of each, and God of all? [123]

In speaking of the "egoism" of Moritz,[124] Béguin says that here
we put our finger on the fundamental sentiment that Moritz had
in common with the Romantics and with German idealism. But,
like Coleridge and Rimbaud, Moritz was unable

to appropriate this feeling, to make of it the very center of his vision
of the Universe, in short, to transform into an instrument of metaphysical conquest what began as an uneasiness or a disease of his
consciousness of self and of the world.

Coleridge made the effort—the history of his philosophical trans-
formations is, taken in one way, the history thereof—but he was
unable to come to rest in Spinoza, in Berkeley, or, finally, in
Kantian idealism. He could not

utilize his illness, in the way a Novalis could, and in the way a
Nerval tried so desperately to do. This act of will, of overcoming,
was not given to Moritz [nor to Coleridge]. And no more was there
given to him that appeasement of inquietude in which a Tieck [or,
we might add, a Wordsworth] gently grew old.[125]

But whether the deviation take the form of an attempt at absolute creation or of an attempt to become pure instrument, the
result is bitter disappointment. "The conclusion," says Maritain,

enunciated with an astonishing lucidity in *A Season in Hell*, was
inevitable. Poetry, aiming, in order to realize itself in full plenitude,
to deliver itself from every condition of existence, poetic knowledge
exalting itself to the point of claiming *absolute* life, engages itself in
a dialectic which kills it. It wants to be everything and give every-

---

[123] *Poems*, p. 102.
[124] See in this book p. 184.
[125] *L'Ame Romantique*, I, 64-65.

thing, the act, sanctity, transsubstantiation, the miracle; it has charge
of humanity. And whatever it does, it is limited by nature, in reality,
to one line only, a particular and very humble one indeed, to the line
of art and of the work-to-be-made. In the end there is nothing left but
to lapse into silence, to renounce the work and poetry at the same
time. Rimbaud not only stopped writing, he avenged himself on
poetry, applied himself to casting it from him as a monster.[126]

"Dejection" sets forth the inevitable conclusion with less astonishing lucidity than *A Season in Hell,* and there is no evidence that
Coleridge ever came to understand so explicitly as Rimbaud what
had happened to him—it would be more than astonishing if he
had. And the conclusion itself was less definitive in Coleridge's
case—he did not cease to write, and far from rejecting poetry and
seeking to revenge himself upon it, he never ceased to feel a sharp
nostalgia for it.

And he was never able really to "utilize his illness," to transform it into "an instrument of metaphysical conquest." Lack of
will, yes, and Coleridge has been taken to task for it by a wide
variety of critics, beginning with himself, with Carlyle following
close on his heels. But also, as Sara Coleridge puts it, a genius
which "was ever impelling him to trace things down to their
deepest source, and follow them out to their remotest ramifications,"[127] a "moral thirst after Truth—the ideal truth—in his own
mind,"[128] and an inability to rest in contradiction, however much
doing so might have appeased his inquietudes, in the manner of
Wordsworth, or of Hartley.[129] In 1824 Coleridge characterized
his *Confessions of an Inquiring Spirit* in this fashion:

the . . . Confessions of one who is neither fair nor saintly, but who—
groaning under a deep sense of infirmity and manifold imperfection—

126 *Situation of Poetry,* pp. 112-13.
127 Quoted by Armour and Howes, *Coleridge the Talker,* p. 29.
128 H. N. Coleridge, quoted *ibid.,* p. 148.
129 See Muirhead, *Coleridge as Philosopher,* p. 42.

feels the want, the necessity, of religious support;—who cannot afford
to lose any the smallest buttress, but who not only loves Truth even
for itself, and when it reveals itself aloof from all interest, but who
loves it with an indescribable awe, which too often withdraws the
genial sap of his activity from the columnar trunk, the sheltering
leaves, the bright and fragrant flower, and the foodful or medicinal
fruitage, to the deep root, ramifying in obscurity and labyrinthine
way-winning—

> In darkness there to house unknown,
> Far underground,
> Pierc'd by no sound
> Save such as live in Fancy's ear alone,
> That listens for the uptorn mandrake's parting groan!

I should be a happier—at all events a more useful—man if my mind
were otherwise constituted. But so it is: and even with regard to
Christianity itself, like certain plants, I creep towards the light, even
though it draw me away from the more nourishing warmth.[130]

As Béguin says of Gérard de Nerval, so we might say of Coleridge, that he was

too much in love with truth, had too lucid an intelligence, to console
himself with illusions. The myths and images which he so loved to
interlace into an immense dream—'I brought my love away like a
prey into solitude'—revealed to him only their delusive unreality.
After each of his explorations in the land of dream, he found himself
more keenly aware of his *échec,* prey to a naked consciousness of his
impotence, to the unappeasable torment of *another* desire—of a desire
to which he would have liked so much to give its real name.[131]

The fantastic yet eminently comprehensible career of Nerval
ended in serious mental illness and suicide. Having made a des-

---

[130] Ed. by H. N. Coleridge (London: William Pickering, 1849), pp. 3-4. Miss
Coburn has entitled an anthology of short prose items from Coleridge's notebooks
and elsewhere *Inquiring Spirit,* and it is a fine epithet for Coleridge if it is understood in the sense that I believe it carries in Coleridge's own title, the confessions
of a man insatiably following out the truth, rather than in a sense perhaps more
current, that of a man of "intellectual curiosity."

[131] *Gérard de Nerval,* 2d ed. (Paris: José Corti, 1955), pp. 97-98.

perate attempt to find ultimate fulfillment through the world of
dreams, through love, and through the poetic experience, and
having failed, he found it no longer possible to live. Coleridge's
échec was less decisive in its results, although, as we have seen,
its effects upon various departments of his life were scarcely less
profound. There is evidence that he finally came to be able to
call his desire for salvation by its true name. A few days before
his death, he wrote to his godson Adam Steinmetz:

And I thus, on the brink of the grave, solemnly bear witness to you,
that the almighty Redeemer, most gracious in his promises to them
that truly seek him, is faithful to perform what He has promised;
and has reserved, under all pains and infirmities, the peace that passeth all understanding, with the supporting assurance of a reconciled
God, who will not withdraw His spirit from me in the conflict, and in
His own time will deliver me from the evil one. Oh, my dear god-
child! eminently blessed are they who begin *early* to seek, to fear, and
love their God, trusting wholly in the righteousness and mediation of
their Lord, Redeemer, Saviour, and everlasting High Priest, Jesus
Christ.[132]

A deepened understanding both of what happened to Coleridge
and of Coleridge's place in the Romantic movement can be
achieved by viewing him in this perspective—as a man engaged
not fearlessly but courageously and with great honesty in an all-
or-nothing struggle—not only to find his relation to an Absolute
but also to understand as clearly as possible what that relation
was; and this at a moment when new spiritual frontiers were
being probed and unique discoveries being made, especially in the
realm of poetic experience and general reflexive awareness, discoveries accompanied by all "the terrors and the promises of
spiritual growth."[133] It has often appeared necessary to excuse or
gloss over the anomalies in Coleridge's life and in his career as

[132] *Letters*, II, 776 (July 13, 1834).
[133] *Biographia Literaria*, II, 216.

poet and thinker. In this context, comparing him with some of his peers, these, no less than his positive achievements, become clear indications of his stature. Although his best poetry stands well enough by itself, a good many of his poems acquire an additional interest when they are read as the records of an heroic quest. It is certainly unnecessary to conceive of him as a person inexplicably divided into two—a towering genius in occasional flashes on the one hand, and an ineffectual, even abject failure on the other. Without glossing over his failures, the case may rest with Coleridge's own words: "By what I *have* effected, am I to be judged by my fellow men; what I *could* have done, is a question for my own conscience."[134] The quest we have been following in these pages may be numbered among the things he *has* effected, and it places him among the foremost of his contemporaries, among those who sacrificed most in the effort to push back the frontiers of human consciousness. In this perspective he is, among Englishmen, perhaps the greatest Romantic.

[134] *Biographia Literaria*, I, 151.

APPENDIX

"Dejection: An Ode" was originally written, on April 4, 1802, in the form of a verse letter to Sara Hutchinson, Wordsworth's sister-in-law, and never published in this form during Coleridge's lifetime. Several much abridged versions were published by Coleridge, of which the final one, which appeared in the 1834 edition of his poems, is given here. For detailed information concerning the history of the poem, see T. M. Raysor, "Coleridge and Asra," *Studies in Philology,* XXVI (1929), 304-24; and George Whalley, *Coleridge and Sara Hutchinson and the Asra Poems* (London: Routledge & Kegan Paul Ltd., 1955).

DEJECTION: AN ODE

> Late, late yestreen I saw the new Moon,
> With the old Moon in her arms;
> And I fear, I fear, my Master dear!
> We shall have a deadly storm.
> *Ballad of Sir Patrick Spence*

I

Well! If the Bard was weather-wise, who made
    The grand old ballad of Sir Patrick Spence,
    This night, so tranquil now, will not go hence
Unroused by winds, that ply a busier trade
Than those which mould yon cloud in lazy flakes,
Or the dull sobbing draft, that moans and rakes
Upon the strings of this Æolian lute,

Which better far were mute.
For lo! the New-moon winter-bright!
10   And overspread with phantom light,
(With swimming phantom light o'erspread
But rimmed and circled by a silver thread)
I see the old Moon in her lap, foretelling
The coming-on of rain and squally blast.
And oh! that even now the gust were swelling,
And the slant night-shower driving loud and fast!
Those sounds which oft have raised me, whilst they awed,
And sent my soul abroad,
Might now perhaps their wonted impulse give,
20   Might startle this dull pain, and make it move and live!

II

A grief without a pang, void, dark, and drear,
A stifled, drowsy, unimpassioned grief,
Which finds no natural outlet, no relief,
In word, or sigh, or tear—
O Lady! in this wan and heartless mood,
To other thoughts by yonder throstle woo'd,
All this long eve, so balmy and serene,
Have I been gazing on the western sky,
And its peculiar tint of yellow green:
30   And still I gaze—and with how blank an eye!
And those thin clouds above, in flakes and bars,
That give away their motion to the stars;
Those stars, that glide behind them or between,
Now sparkling, now bedimmed, but always seen:
Yon crescent Moon, as fixed as if it grew
In its own cloudless, starless lake of blue;
I see them all so excellently fair,
I see, not feel, how beautiful they are!

III

My genial spirits fail;
40   And what can these avail

To lift the smothering weight from off my breast?
    It were a vain endeavor,
    Though I should gaze forever
On that green light that lingers in the west:
I may not hope from outward forms to win
The passion and the life, whose fountains are within.

IV

O Lady! we receive but what we give,
And in our life alone does Nature live:
Ours is her wedding garment, ours her shroud!
50   And would we aught behold, of higher worth,
Than that inanimate cold world allowed
To the poor loveless ever-anxious crowd,
    Ah! from the soul itself must issue forth
A light, a glory, a fair luminous cloud
      Enveloping the Earth—
And from the soul itself must there be sent
    A sweet and potent voice, of its own birth,
Of all sweet sounds the life and element!

V

O pure of heart! thou need'st not ask of me
60 What this strong music in the soul may be!
What, and wherein it doth exist,
This light, this glory, this fair luminous mist,
This beautiful and beauty-making power.
    Joy, virtuous Lady! Joy that ne'er was given,
Save to the pure, and in their purest hour,
Life, and Life's effluence, cloud at once and shower,
Joy, Lady! is the spirit and the power,
Which wedding Nature to us gives in dower
    A new Earth and new Heaven,
70 Undreamt of by the sensual and the proud—
Joy is the sweet voice, Joy the luminous cloud—
    We in ourselves rejoice!

And thence flows all that charms or ear or sight,
    All melodies the echoes of that voice,
All colours a suffusion from that light.

VI

There was a time when, though my path was rough,
    This joy within me dallied with distress,
And all misfortunes were but as the stuff
    Whence Fancy made me dreams of happiness:
80 For hope grew round me, like the twining vine,
And fruits, and foliage, not my own, seemed mine.
But now afflictions bow me down to earth:
Nor care I that they rob me of my mirth;
    But oh! each visitation
Suspends what nature gave me at my birth,
    My shaping spirit of Imagination.
For not to think of what I needs must feel,
    But to be still and patient, all I can;
And haply by abstruse research to steal
90   From my own nature all the natural man—
This was my sole resource, my only plan:
Till that which suits a part infects the whole,
And now is almost grown the habit of my soul.

VII

Hence, viper thoughts, that coil around my mind,
    Reality's dark dream!
I turn from you, and listen to the wind,
    Which long has raved unnoticed. What a scream
Of agony by torture lengthened out
That lute sent forth! Thou Wind, that rav'st without,
100   Bare crag, or mountain-tairn, or blasted tree,
Or pine-grove whither woodman never clomb,
Or lonely house, long held the witches' home,
    Methinks were fitter instruments for thee,
Mad Lutanist! who in this month of showers,
Of dark-brown gardens, and of peeping flowers,

Mak'st Devils' yule, with worse than wintry song,
The blossoms, buds, and timorous leaves among.
    Thou Actor, perfect in all tragic sounds!
Thou mighty Poet, e'en to frenzy bold!
110   What tell'st thou now about?
     'Tis of the rushing of an host in rout,
      With groans, of trampled men, with smarting wounds—
At once they groan with pain, and shudder with the cold!
But hush!. there is a pause of deepest silence!
    And all that noise, as of a rushing crowd,
With groans, and tremulous shudderings—all is over—
     It tells another tale, with sounds less deep and loud!
      A tale of less affright,
      And tempered with delight,
120 As Otway's self had framed the tender lay,—
      'Tis of a little child
      Upon a lonesome wild,
Not far from home, but she hath lost her way;
And now moans low in bitter grief and fear,
And now screams loud, and hopes to make her mother hear.

VIII

'Tis midnight, but small thoughts have I of sleep:
Full seldom may my friend such vigils keep!
Visit her, gentle Sleep! with wings of healing,
    And may this storm be but a mountain-birth,
130 May all the stars hang bright above her dwelling,
     Silent as though they watched the sleeping Earth!
      With light heart may she rise,
      Gay fancy, cheerful eyes,
    Joy lift her spirit, joy attune her voice;
To her may all things live, from pole to pole,
Their life the eddying of her living soul!
     O simple spirit, guided from above,
Dear Lady! friend devoutest of my choice,
Thus mayest thou ever, evermore rejoice.

BIBLIOGRAPHY

WORKS BY COLERIDGE

Aids to Reflection, in *Complete Works.* Vol. I.

Anima Poetae, ed. by E. H. Coleridge. London: Wm. Heinemann, 1895.

Biographia Literaria, ed. by J. Shawcross. London: Oxford University Press, 1939.

Complete Works, ed. by W. G. T. Shedd. New York: Harper & Bros., 1871-76.

Confessions of an Inquiring Spirit and Some Miscellaneous Pieces, ed. by H. N. Coleridge. London: Pickering, 1849.

The Friend, in *Complete Works.* Vol. II.

A Lay Sermon, Addressed to the Higher and Middle Classes on the Existing Distresses and Discontents, in *Complete Works.* Vol. VI.

Letters of Samuel Taylor Coleridge, ed. by E. H. Coleridge. Boston & New York: Houghton, Mifflin, 1895.

Letters, Conversations, and Recollections, ed. by Thomas Alsop. London: Frederick Farrah, 1864.

Notes, Theological, Political, and Miscellaneous, ed. by Derwent Coleridge. London: Ed. Moxon, 1853.

Philosophical Lectures, ed. by Kathleen Coburn. New York: Philosophical Library, 1949.

The Poems of Samuel Taylor Coleridge, ed. by E. H. Coleridge. London: Oxford University Press, 1945.

Specimens of the Table Talk of Samuel Taylor Coleridge, ed. by H. N. Coleridge. London: John Murray, 1851.

The Statesman's Manual; or the Bible, the Best Guide to Political Skill and Foresight: A Lay Sermon, Addressed to the Higher Classes of Society, in *Complete Works.* Vol. I.

Theory of Life, in *Complete Works.* Vol. I.

Unpublished Letters of Samuel Taylor Coleridge including Certain Letters Republished from Original Sources, ed. by Earl Leslie Griggs. London: Constable & Co. Ltd., 1932.

GENERAL REFERENCES

Abrams, M. H., *The Mirror and the Lamp.* New York: W. W. Norton, 1958.

Alsop, Thomas. *See under* "Works by Coleridge."

Armour, Richard W., and Raymond F. Howes, *Coleridge the Talker.* Ithaca: Cornell University Press, 1940.

Aynard, Joseph, "Notes inédites de Coleridge," *Revue Germanique,* VII (1911), 301-17.

Baudelaire, Charles, *Mon Coeur Mis à Nu,* in *Oeuvres Posthumes,* ed. by Eugène Crépit. Paris: Maison Quantin, 1887.

Béguin, Albert, *L'Ame Romantique et le Rêve, Essai sur le Romantisme Allemand et la Poésie Française.* Marseille: Editions des Cahiers du Sud, 1937.

—— *Gérard de Nerval, suivi de Poésie et Mystique.* Paris: Librairie Stock, 1936.

—— *Gérard de Nerval.* 2d ed. Paris: José Corti, 1945.

Beres, David, "A Dream, a Vision, and a Poem: a Psychoanalytic Study of the Origins of the *Rime of the Ancient Mariner,*" *International Journal of Psycho-Analysis,* XXXII, No. 2 (1951), 97-116.

Bewley, Marius, "The Poetry of Coleridge," *Scrutiny,* VIII (March, 1940), 406-20.

Bliss, H. S., and D. T. Bliss, "Coleridge's 'Kubla Kahn,'" *American Imago,* VI, No. 4 (1949), 261-73.

Bonjour, Adrien, *Coleridge's "Hymn Before Sunrise"; a Study of Facts and Problems Connected with the Poem.* Lausanne: Imprimerie La Concorde, 1942.

Brooke, Stopford, *Theology in the English Poets.* London: J. M. Dent & Sons, 1874.

Brooks, Cleanth, *The Well-Wrought Urn.* New York: Reynal & Hitchcock, 1947.

Campbell, James Dykes, *Samuel Taylor Coleridge, a Narrative of the Events in his Life.* London and New York: Macmillan, 1894.

Carus, Karl Gustav, *Psyche, zur Entwicklungsgeschichte der Seele.* Pforzheim: Flammer & Hoffman, 1846.

Child, Francis J., *English and Scottish Ballads.* Boston: Houghton, Mifflin & Co., 1860.

Coburn, Kathleen, *Inquiring Spirit, a New Presentation of Coleridge from his Published and Unpublished Prose Writings.* London: Routledge and Paul, 1951.

—— *See also* "Works by Coleridge."

Coleridge, Derwent. *See under* "Works by Coleridge."

Coleridge, E. H. *See under* "Works by Coleridge."

Coleridge, H. N. *See under* "Works by Coleridge."

Cottle, Joseph, *Early Recollections, chiefly Relating to Samuel Taylor Coleridge.* London: Longmans, 1837.

Eliot, T. S., "The Frontiers of Criticism," *Sewanee Review,* Vol. LXVI (1956).

—— *Selected Essays.* New ed. New York: Harcourt Brace, 1950.

Etiemble, René, *Le Mythe de Rimbaud.* Paris: Gallimard, 1952-54.

Fairchild, H. N., *Religious Trends in English Poetry.* New York: Columbia University Press, 1949.

Garrod, H. W., "Dejection: an Ode, 67-70. Punctuation," *Times Literary Supplement* (May 4, 1922), p. 308.

Gilson, Etienne, *The Spirit of Medieval Philosophy.* New York: Scribners, 1936.

Gingerich, S. F., "From Necessity to Transcendentalism in Coleridge," *Publications of the Modern Language Association,* XXXV (1920), 1-59.

Griggs, Leslie. *See under* "Works by Coleridge."

Hackett, Carl A., *Rimbaud.* London: Bowes & Bowes, 1957.

Hanson, Lawrence, *The Life of S. T. Coleridge, the Early Years.* London: G. Allen & Unwin, 1938.

Howes, Raymond F. *See* Armour and Howes.

House, Humphrey, *Coleridge.* London: Rupert Hart-Davis, 1953.

James, D. G., *Romantic Comedy.* New York and London: Oxford University Press, 1948.

Knight, G. Wilson, *The Starlit Dome, Studies in the Poetry of Vision*. London: Oxford University Press, 1941.

Lowes, John Livingston, *The Road to Xanadu*. Boston and New York: Houghton, Mifflin & Co., 1927.

Maritain, Jacques, *Art and Scholasticism*. New York: Scribners, 1930.

—— *Distinguer pour Unir, ou les Degrés du Savoir*. Paris: Desclée de Brouwer, 1940.

—— and Raïssa Maritain, *The Situation of Poetry*. New York: Philosophical Library, 1955.

Muirhead, J. H., *Coleridge as Philosopher*. London: Macmillan, 1930.

—— "Metaphysician or Mystic," in *Coleridge, Studies by Several Hands on the Hundredth Anniversary of his Death*, ed. by Edmund Blunden and Earl Leslie Griggs. London: Constable, 1934.

Nerval, Gérard de, *Oeuvres Choisies*. Lausanne: Henri Kaeser, 1948.

Nettesheim, Josephine, "Das Erlöschen von Coleridges 'dichterischer Produktion' um 1800," *Archiv für das Studium der neueren Sprachen und Literaturen*, CXLVI (1923), 213-22.

Nidecker, Henri, "Notes Marginales de S. T. Coleridge," *Revue de Littérature Comparée*, VII (1927), 336-48.

Plotinus, *The Ethical Treatises*, trans. by Stephen Mackenna. London and Boston: The Medici Society, 1926.

Ransom, John Crowe, *Collected Poems*. New York: Alfred Knopf, 1945.

Renéville, Rolland de, *Rimbaud le Voyant*. Paris: Au Sans Pareil, 1929.

Richards, Ivor A., *Coleridge on Imagination*. New York: W. W. Norton, 1950.

—— "Coleridge the Vulnerable Poet," *Yale Review*, XLVIII (New Series: June, 1959), 491-504.

Rimbaud, Arthur, *La Lettre du Voyant*, in *Un Coeur sous un Soutane, précédé de La Lettre du Voyant*. Paris: Presses du Livre Français, 1950.

—— *Oeuvres*. Paris: Mercure de France, 1947.

Schneider, Elisabeth, *Coleridge, Opium, and 'Kubla Khan.'* Chicago: University of Chicago Press, 1953.

Shawcross, J. *See under* "Works by Coleridge."

Shedd, W. G. T. *See under* "Works by Coleridge."

Snyder, Alice D., "Coleridge on Giordano Bruno," *Modern Language Notes,* XLII (1927), 427-36.

Starkie, Enid, *Arthur Rimbaud.* New York: W. W. Norton, 1947.

Stewart, Herbert, "The Place of Coleridge in English Theology," *Harvard Theological Review,* Vol. XVIII (1918).

Storr, V. F., *Development of English Theology in the Nineteenth Century, 1800-1860.* London and New York: Longmans, Green, 1913.

Tate, Allen, *The Forlorn Demon.* Chicago: Regnery, 1953.

Tulloch, John, *Movements of Religious Thought in Britain in the Nineteenth Century.* London: Longmans, 1885.

Van Leeuwen, Anton, "L'Analogie de l'Etre," *Revue Néoscholastique de Philosophie,* XXXIX (1936), 293-320.

Warren, Robert Penn, "A Poem of Pure Imagination, an Experiment in Reading," in *The Rime of the Ancient Mariner, with an Essay by Robert Penn Warren.* New York: Reynal & Hitchcock, 1946.

Whalley, George, *Coleridge and Sara Hutchinson and the Asra Poems.* London: Routledge & Kegan Paul Ltd., 1955.

Wilson, John, "The Late James Smith," *Blackwood's Magazine,* XLVIII (1840), 361-73.

Winkelmann, Elisabeth, *Coleridge und die kantische Philosophie.* Leipzig: Mayer & Muller, 1933.

Wordsworth, William, Preface to the Second Edition of *Lyrical Ballads,* in *The Poetical Works of Wordsworth,* ed. by T. Hutchinson. London: Oxford University Press, 1932.

Yeats, William Butler, *Collected Poems.* New York: Macmillan, 1942.

INDEX

N.C.   Suther, Marshall Edward
821.09   The dark night of Samuel
S   Taylor Coleridge.

Wilmington Public Library
Wilmington, N. C.

RULES

1. Books marked 7 days may be kept one week. Books marked 14 days, two weeks. The latter may be renewed, if more than 6 months old.

2. A fine of two cents a day will be charged on each book which is not returned according to the above rule. No book will be issued to any person having a fine of 25 cents or over.

3. A charge of ten cents will be made for mutilated plastic jackets. All injuries to books beyond reasonable wear and all losses shall be made good to the satisfaction of the Librarian.

4. Each borrower is held responsible for all books drawn on his card and for all fines accruing on the same.